Revised First Edition

FIRST
THINGS
FIRST

FOUNDATIONAL
TOOLS FOR
COLLEGIATE WRITING

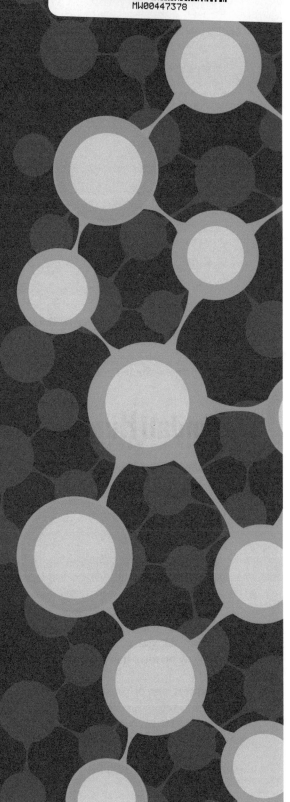

JOLINE SCOTT-ROLLER

Kendall Hunt
publishing company

CONTENTS

DEDICATION

To my students, for being great teachers
and
To Nolan and Grace for being my inspiration and motivation

ACKNOWLEDGMENTS

So many people are behind this text and deserve some notes of thanks! Katie and Michelle, my editors, thank you for being so understanding and helpful! My colleagues, who helped me figure out what it was I wanted to do with this project: Susan Blake and Vicki Schwaab. My mentors, who not only helped me learn what it was to be a "good" teacher, but supported me in everything I tried: Gary Levine and Christine Vodicka. And much thanks, as always, goes to Bruce for making sure I had the time and sanity to get it all done!

For the second edition, thanks go to Dr. Maura Grady for her support and championing, as well as Emily Weller for her expertise in course design. My gratitude also goes out to Ashland University and especially to Mary Deloe for their support of this text.

INTRO

So you're not so great at English. That's okay, I'm not so good at math. In fact, when I went to college, I had to take remedial math: basically, high school math all over again. The great thing is, over the years, I have practiced my math and am glad to say that today I can actually calculate a grade in my head faster than I can on a calculator! See, skills like math and English aren't something you're either "good" at or "bad" at. They are, like any skill, ones that you have either practiced or haven't. True, some people do seem to have a "natural inclination" for one or the other, but just because you're a "math person" doesn't mean that you can't learn how to write really well.

Writing an essay is, in many ways, like learning to ride a bike or to shoot a basketball or to draw; it is a skill that you must actually practice in order to learn. You really cannot read a book about writing and then know how to write. This is why you take a class in college with a professor. The assignments are your practice. The class is guidance for your practice. Your professor is alignment for that practice, someone to help you identify where you've gone wrong and how to correct yourself. Hopefully, no matter how you felt about writing and reading and English in general in high school, or previous to taking this course, you will come to understand and accept that there is nothing wrong with starting at the beginning, in basics. After all, doesn't that make sense?

So, why is it so hard to write formally?

In this class, you will be learning how to write academically. That means something specific. It is different than writing creatively (although there are classes for that and I highly recommend them!), and it is different than writing randomly (a note or email, for example). Writing academically means that you are using a defined method of organization and a formal tone. And that is exactly why academic writing is hard to do!

Some people ask, "I have been using English my whole life, why can't I write?" You can blame your brain for that. The brain processes language in many different areas, and unfortunately, none of those areas has direct communication with another! The areas of your brain that process heard and spoken English have the most practice; after all, you've been listening to English since you were in the womb (if English is your first language) and you've been speaking English since you were probably around two years old. You both listen to and speak English constantly, all day, every day. Maybe even in your sleep. However, you didn't start writing English until much later, and you do not spend anywhere near the amount of time writing English that you do hearing and speaking it. So, the area of your brain that processes writing English is not very practiced.

Like learning to ride a bike or shoot a basketball, you need to build up the right neural pathways to write. That is why practicing is so important, and why you will be asked to practice writing a lot in this class. Eventually, after a semester or two or three, you will have built up enough neural pathways that you will no longer have to think as hard about writing, the same way that you no longer have to think so hard about how to ride a bike. The methods you will learn will become engrained, and writing an essay will not seem so daunting. It may even seem easy!

Am I actually going to use this book?

The short answer is: Yes! This is a workbook and it therefore contains almost everything that you will be doing for the semester (readings may be external). If you complete all of the assignments and you put the effort of thought into them that you should, you will leave this class ready to move on to the next level of English course. Hopefully, you will also leave feeling confident in your abilities as a writer!

Good luck!
~Joline

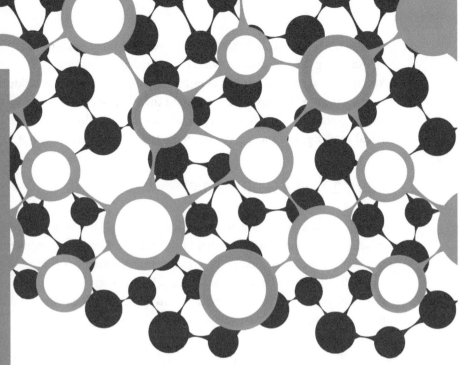

LESSON ONE

Annotation

Before you walk, you must crawl. Before you can add, you must count. And before you can write, you must read. Reading, at least in college for the purpose of classes, cannot be done passively. It is not enough to be able to tell what something *said*; you must be able to tell what it *meant*. For example, look at the word here:

Autumn

You should have no problem identifying the word. You could easily read it aloud. You know what it *says*. Now, write what the word *means*.

_____

_____

_____

You can, obviously, read English (duh, because you're reading this now!) but so much of reading is about being able to discern what is not in black and white on the page. In college, you will be asked to read something, think about it, formulate questions and ideas based on it, and then relate it to something else. This is very different than being asked to simply remember what you read and answer questions, and when you are first learning to do it, it can be difficult. We call this process **critical reading**, and there are some tools to help you accomplish it.

Reading Tool #1: Chunking

Do you consider yourself a poor or slow reader? Have you ever read something and thought to yourself, "Wow, I have no idea what I just read," and then find yourself rereading it, maybe multiple times? This is a common issue. It is important to remember that reading is not a race. Some people get the idea that they have to read quickly in order to be considered a "good" reader, but that's not right! The goal of reading is to understand and remember what you have read, and if you can, no matter how long it takes you, then you are a "good" reader!

Imagine that I am holding a paper cup and that I use a pencil to poke a hole in the bottom. Then, I start pouring water into the cup. As long as I pour the water slowly and evenly, the water comes out the bottom through the hole and goes wherever I want it to. But what happens if I simply dump a whole bunch of water into the cup? Sure, some will go through the hole in the bottom, but most of it is going to just spill out everywhere, going nowhere. Right? Your brain works similarly; it can only process so much information at once before it gets overloaded and loses most of it.

In psychology, there is a memory tool called **chunking**, which refers to the process of splitting information up into pieces, or chunks, that are easier to process. When you are reading, you can chunk the text into manageable parts. That may be different for everyone; some people can read for an hour and others can only read for 15 minutes before they have to stop and let their brain process. You will have to determine how much information you can process at once. One clue is to be aware of when you become distracted. Maybe you start to notice the squirrel in the tree out your window, or maybe you start to wonder what you'll have for dinner, or maybe your leg starts to bounce. This is when you need to take a break. But, your brain works really, really fast, so a break doesn't have to be long. Count to 30. Go to the bathroom, or get a drink. Maybe do a few jumping jacks or push-ups, even. DO NOT add extra information to the load for your brain to process! That means no watching TV, no going on Facebook, and no texting!

So, now you have a tool for how to slow down your reading so that you can remember and process what you've read, but how do you start to understand and analyze what you've read to come up with questions and ideas?

JOURNAL 1

Write one page about your previous writing experience.
For example: What kind of writing did you do in high school? Do
you like writing/reading? Why? Try to give specific examples.

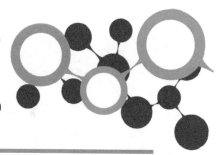

Reading Tool #2: Annotation

Annotation is the process of interacting with a text by highlighting, writing marginal notes, and otherwise marking up the pages. This process has many benefits and serves several purposes. Annotating is the best tool to use to teach your brain how to read critically because it forces you to analyze and process as you read. It forces you to read more slowly, therefore giving your brain more time to filter the information into your working or long-term memory. Other reasons to annotate are:

1. For reference. Highlighting or otherwise marking important information or concepts in a text make them easy to find again. In class when you're asked a question, or later when you want to refer to something specific while writing your essay, you won't waste valuable time flipping through pages, skimming paragraphs trying to find what you're looking for.

2. To record initial reactions. We all have some thoughts while we read, whether those thoughts are "Wow, this is really boring" and "This author is a total idiot" to "Geeze, that's disgusting" or even "Hmm, interesting." These reactions should be written, in some form, in the margins. They may take the form of symbols, like question marks, or doodles or actual words. It doesn't matter what form your marginal notes take, as long as you understand what they mean.

3. To make connections. Marginal notes can also serve as a method of making connections between ideas. I find arrows to be especially useful, drawing them between pieces of information that connect. You may also write questions or reference other texts, lectures, movies, or any other form of information in marginal notes.

Highlighting and marginal notes are not the only types of annotation. You can also underline, circle, or star things with a pen. You could use post-it notes or tabs to mark certain pages or passages, or even dog-ear your pages. The definition of annotation specifically uses the word "interact" because annotation requires you to become physically involved with the pages, and therefore the information. You'd be surprised at the amount of research out there that shows how much better you remember things if you can assign a physicality to it!

PRACTICE EXERCISE #1: GRAMMAR—DIAGNOSTIC

Having a hammer doesn't do you any good unless you've had practice hitting a nail with it, so let's practice using this new tool. Annotate the article your instructor has provided for you, being sure to note not only vocabulary you may be unfamiliar with and important facts, but also what connections you make or thoughts you have while reading.

Complete the following diagnostic to help determine your grammar level.
Directions: Identify **_and_** correct the mistake.

1. Going to the fair. Will be fun this year. With my friends. _____

   _____

2. I like to eat the food at the fair and I like to see the animals but my favorite thing to do is to ride on the Ferris wheel you should come with me.

   _____

   _____

3. I am going to enter my strawberry jam into the contest at the fair, I hope I win a blue ribbon!

_____

_____

4. I went to the fair to eat cobbler wearing my best white shirt.

_____

_____

5. Is you going to purchase a pass for all of the rides at the fair?

_____

_____

6. Lucy and Beth are going to her booth to help Sara prepare her horse.

_____

_____

7. We drove to the fair but walking home.

_____

_____

8. All of the participant/participants/participants' entries should have been judged by now.

_____

_____

9. How does/did/do you know where to find the exhibits you were looking for?

_____

_____

10. You should go to the horse show to see Mark/Marks/Mark's new riding routine.

_____

_____

PRACTICE EXERCISE #2: SENTENCE SUITCASES

We've done a lot of work with reading skills, so now let us put them to the test. The following quotation is fairly complex. Read the sentence, then write out the meaning of each phrase in your own words. At the end, rewrite the sentence in your own words so that it has the same meaning as the original.

© Danny Smyth/Shuttestock.com

"When in the course of human events it becomes necessary for one people to dissolve the political bands which have connected them with another, and to assume among the powers of the earth, the separate and equal station to which the Laws of Nature and of Nature's God entitle them, a decent respect to the opinions of mankind requires that they should declare the causes which impel them to the separation"

~The Declaration of Independence, Thomas Jefferson

1. "When in the course of human events" -

_____

_____

2. "…it becomes necessary for one people to dissolve the political bands which have connected them with another…" -

_____

_____

3. "…and to assume among the powers of earth…" -

_____

_____

4. "…the separate and equal station to which the Laws of Nature and of Nature's God entitle them…" -

_____

_____

5. "…a decent respect to the opinions of mankind requires that they should declare the causes which impel them to the separation." -

_____

_____

ESSAY 1

Essay Mode—Summary

Why go around hammering nails into things for no reason? Using a tool, like annotation or an outline, is rather pointless unless you're using it to *create* something. We use hammer and nails to hold things together, everything from birdhouses to houses for people, and many things in between. Similarly, we can use annotation, outlines, thesis statements, and other writing tools to build different types of essays. There are many types, or modes, of essays you might be asked to write in college. Sometimes an essay prompt or assignment might even require you to combine modes. It is important, therefore, for you to understand the basic types of essays, their purposes, and functions. As always, first things first: The most basic type of essay is a summary.

Now, you are probably familiar with the word "summary." You may have heard or read it in passing, or you may even (hopefully!) have heard a teacher use the word in the past. Oftentimes in elementary school, what is called a "book report" is really just a summary. A **summary** is simply a retelling of something, written or otherwise, in a shorter form, using different words. A summary should always hit the same points, in the same order, as the original form.

The tricky part about doing a summary is deciding just what information is important and what isn't. You want to convey to another person the vital parts of the original without giving all of the detail that the original did. Let's try this out.

PRACTICE EXERCISE #1

On the lines provided, write a short summary of one of your favorite movies. Make sure you hit all the major information, but make sure it all fits in this space!

_____

_____

_____

_____

_____

What kind of information did you provide? There were many options. For example, did you write about the main characters? Did you provide their names or important details about them, like their occupations? Did you provide all of the major plot points of the film, including backstory or conclusion? You may have provided information about the setting (city, time period, etc.), or whether the film was a comedy, a romance, or an action movie. That would all be considered important information, but it still leaves out some other vital details. For example, when was the movie released, who were the actors in it, and who directed it? This is identification information and it is important to include.

As you wrote this summary, you had to decide many things, and you did so very quickly and intuitively. Your brain works unconsciously much more quickly than it does consciously. For example, you had to decide what information you were going to provide and in what order to provide it. You probably didn't sit for an hour trying to decide how to do that. Instead, you borrowed from the original source, providing what your brain deemed "vital" in the same order that the original did. Good for you! That is exactly how a summary is supposed to work!

Essay Mode—Critique

A summary is a retelling, so it doesn't include any *new* information. In a summary, there is no room for anything other than the main points from the original source. A critique is the next step, adding a layer of information that was not included in the original source. You may be familiar with the word "critique"—it is related to the word "criticism," and our culture is full of that! A formal critique, though, has a purpose, which is to evaluate a particular thing. When we evaluate something, we usually make some kind of judgment about whether the thing was "good" or "bad," and we usually base that judgment on a set of standards that specifically apply to whatever it is we are evaluating.

Now, that all is a bit abstract and confusing, so let's practice with something that is a little more familiar. In the lines provided, make a list of some things you might talk about if someone asked you to tell them whether a movie you'd recently seen was "good" or "bad."

_____

_____

_____

_____

_____

_____

For example, many critics agreed that in the Star Wars Prequel Trilogy, the CGI was amazing, the costumes were spectacular, the action was thrilling, and the mythology (all the aliens and different planets, etc.) was deep and rich. However, most critics also agreed that the story was weak, the characters were simpering, the script was mediocre, and the acting was poor. These are all examples of elements that we use to evaluate movies. Your list might have also included elements like musical score, story logic, the lighting, the editing, or other things. These are all elements of construction, of how the movie was made. When you talk or write about these things, you have specific examples you can refer to, information that you use to "back up" what you're claiming. A critique is not just your opinion about something (oh, I hated that movie!), but is an evaluation based on standards and evidence.

PRACTICE EXERCISE #2

Let's try it out. In the lines provided, write a short critique of the same movie you summarized earlier. Remember that just because you liked the movie doesn't necessarily mean that is was made well. (One of my favorite movies is about a dog and a dolphin that become friends, but I can readily admit it's not really a *good* movie.)

_____

_____

_____

_____

_____

_____

_____

So, what kind of elements did you write about? How did you decide which elements to write about? You probably highlighted the elements that stood out—either positively or negatively. That is exactly what a critique is supposed to do: evaluate those specific elements that either meet and exceed standards or seriously miss the standards.

There are standards in writing, too. For the purposes of what we're doing, we're going to look at standards for academic writing; there are different elements and standards to consider when looking at fiction, journalistic writing, or science reports, for example. The elements of academic writing tend to span all kinds of essays you might write in college, although occasionally a particular instructor or course might require you to do something different.

Essay Tool #1: Understanding Mechanics vs. Content

When you are looking at how a piece of writing is constructed, you will have to consider two sets of elements. The first is mechanics, the literal part of "how" something is written. The second part is content, which is more about what is said or how it is said. In the lines provided, make one list of mechanical elements and another list of content elements.

MECHANICS

_____

_____

_____

_____

_____

_____

_____

_____

_____

CONTENT

_____

_____

_____

_____

_____

_____

_____

_____

_____

Summary/Critique

GOALS:

> Demonstrate that you understood and fully comprehended what you read
> Demonstrate that you were able to pick out the main purpose and main supporting points
> Demonstrate an understanding of content and mechanics
> Demonstrate an understanding of academic standards for writing
> Demonstrate a collegiate level of writing (organization, sentence structure, punctuation, etc.)

DIRECTIONS:

Summarize and critique one of the articles provided to you. For the summary, pretend that I have never read the article and you are "telling" me what it says and/or is about. It is important to clearly state the main idea/thesis of the article, as well as the main supporting points. You may include other major information as points of interest or demonstration of an idea. This should be a short part of your full essay, about a third of the body section. For the critique, evaluate whether or not the article is well written based on academic standards. It is important to evaluate content as well as mechanics (organization, sentence structure, vocabulary, etc.). Use specific examples from the article in support or demonstration of your points.

- Nowhere in your essay should you use first person (the words *me*, *my*, or *I*)!

TIPS:

Do's
- Include the name of the author, title of the article, and source.
- Repeat the exact information the author provided.
- Use direct quotes when appropriate.
- Use your own words to repeat what the author wrote.
- Explain ideas that are not explicitly stated.
- Determine the intended audience.
- Determine the author's purpose/goal in writing this article.
- Determine a set of parameters that define "good" vs. "bad" for this mode.

Do Not
- Include any of your own thoughts/ideas.
- Use more than two direct quotes.
- Include any of your own opinions.
- Include information about any other article(s).

REQUIREMENTS:

- _____ words
- One line of direct quote (no more)
- Staple prep work to the back of the rough draft
- Proper formatting (per syllabus)

PRACTICE: STUDENT ESSAY #1

Name:_____

Should you be expected to know how to ride a bike if you had never seen someone do it? Or know how to hammer a nail, throw a ball into a basket, or perform any other kind of skill without first having some kind of demonstration? Of course not, and you shouldn't be expected to know how to write if you have never read. Reading (a lot) is the only other thing than writing that can truly help you to become a better writer. Because we are learning to write in a very specific manner, you need to read examples. For each essay, you will read a student example and complete a worksheet designed to help you learn from the example. Let's get started!

Directions: After reading and annotating the article, complete the worksheet. Detach all of the work from your book, staple together with this worksheet on top, and bring to class.

In yellow, highlight the thesis statement.
In pink, highlight each topic sentence or main point.
In blue, highlight the summarizing or critique words and phrases.
In green, highlight any vocabulary you are unfamiliar with.
Circle with a pen any grammatical or punctuation mistakes you find.

Answer the following:

1. Identify what this essay is summarizing/critiquing.

   _____

   _____

2. Who do you think is the audience for this essay?

   _____

   _____

3. What do you think is the purpose of this essay?

   _____

   _____

4. Do you think this essay achieves the goals of a summary? Why?

    _____

    _____

5. What is the writer's evaluation of the article being critiqued?

    _____

    _____

    _____

    _____

Megan Worthman

Essay 2

25 February 2012

Word Count: 1079

Critical/Rhetorical Analysis Essay

In Ted Spiker's article "How Men Really Feel About Their Bodies," Spiker writes about the issues that men have with their body image. He writes this article at an academic level that most Americans can read. This article is written for men and women who are interested in reading more about how men feel about their bodies. Spiker does a good job writing this article at a level that most people would be able to understand what he is writing about by his organization, sentence structure and the vocabulary used.

Spiker's article is written so that the people who read it will be able to come away with the message that he wants them to. This article was written for *The Oprah Magazine*, which lets his readers know that it came from a reliable source, and most adults will be able to read it without any problems understanding it. His audience is mainly for those who have a reading level of about high school level. The vocabulary that Spiker uses is not complex. This article is actually very readable and the reader will not have to stop and look up words they do not know. His sentences are not very long or complex, which is good because it will not turn the reader away because they are too long or cannot be understood. His sentences flow nicely together and are organized in a way that makes the paper easy to read.

Spiker does a good job organizing the essay so that everything flows together. He does not jump around from topic to topic, which is good. Spiker starts off paragraphs with a topic sentence such as "Seven: Men's body image problems can be just as dangerous as women's," and then goes on to explain that topic sentence in more detail so they reader has more knowledge about what he is trying to get across. His explanations of his topic sentences make sense, he focuses his writing on the topic sentences that we wrote, and he does a good job not leaving his audience wondering what he was trying to get across. He gives a detailed explanation of the main point he wants readers to know, and he does so in a way where he uses quotes from other people or he uses examples from his own life. He starts off his article by saying "At six feet two and 215 pounds, I'm not huge. I just carry my weight where women do-in my hips, butt, and thighs" (Spiker), so when he uses examples from his own life, the readers know that he understands what it is like to be unhappy with a person's body. Doing this is a good way to show the readers that the author has knowledge of what he is writing about, and that makes his audience interested and care about what the author has to say.

The tone that Spiker uses in the article is a tone as if he were speaking to someone. He does not sounds demanding to the audience, he is just trying to inform them of what men go through with their body, for example he writes 8 reasons why or how men treat their bodies ranging from "Instead, we'll joke about our bodies," to "We want to look like we're 25" (Spiker). This article was written to inform his audience of men's body issues, and it does just that. He does a good job in writing the article in a way that does not turn readers away from the article, instead he writes the article in a way that makes his readers want to keep reading. The topics he writes about make sense by themselves, but he goes into detail about each one of them. This gives readers further information about each topic that he put into his article. Each one of his topic sentences is important to the article, and he splits each one of them into their own section so the article does not seem like a run on. He does a good job making sure that each individual paragraph is not too long, but it gives the reader enough information that they can understand what he is talking about. The article itself is not long at all, only 3 pages front and back which encourages his readers to read the article all the way through. His topics flow smoothly throughout the article and he does not jump around and confuse the readers about what he is going to say next. Each source or person he gets information from is reliable such as; Lynne Luciano, Ph.D, who researched body image issues at California State University at Domenguez Hills and he uses examples from his own experience. With the examples he uses it shows his readers he has a good idea on what he is writing about and he is not just making up the information that he puts in his article which makes readers want to read what he has to say. His article is very informative and his readers will come away from it with a new outlook on men and how they view their bodies. In his article he states that "18 percent of men are happy enough with their physiques that they wouldn't change them" (Spiker), which most people may not have known.

In conclusion, Spiker does a good job writing articles at an academic level that most can understand. He makes sure to not use language his audience would not understand and he gives enough detail to back up his topic sentences so the readers have the information that they need to come away with what he wants them too. The sources that he uses in his article are reliable which is good to have because it shows his readers that he does not make up the information in his articles. His organization of his article is good in the way that is splits up each topic into its own paragraph. Doing this makes sure the reader knows that he is moving from topic to topic and is not jumping around without the reader knowing it. The structure of his sentences are not complex which makes this article an easy read. Overall, this article is informative and the readers will come away with the information they may or may not have known that Spiker intended them to come away with.

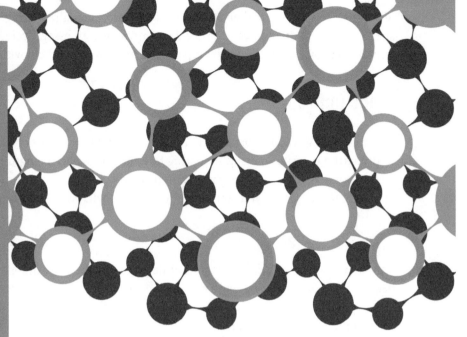

Prep Work

Have you ever had the experience of opening up a Word document and then staring at the blank page, wondering how to start? Or maybe you start typing right away, but later you find that your essay doesn't make much sense because you jumped around from one idea to another. These are common experiences, and they are a result of a lack of preparation. The goal of preparation is to make writing an essay easy! Think of it this way:

>   Thinking about the assignment, reading, and annotating = 85% of the effort of writing

>   Prep work, as in taking notes, concept map, and outline = 10% of the effort of writing

>   Actually sitting down and typing out the essay = 5% of the effort of writing

If you follow this paradigm, you will spend the majority of your effort simply thinking about your essay, some effort organizing all of those thoughts, and then only a little bit of effort actually writing. Hey, you know English—you speak it and read it and hear it every day. Organizing an essay, deciding which material to include and in what order, is really the hard part, and prep work can help with that.

Steps to Prep

Critical reading is an important skill in and of itself, but in terms of academia it is only the first step in preparing to write an essay. Preparing to write an essay is a lengthy process, so it is important to start as soon as you get an assignment. In time, you will train your brain to make these connections by taking these steps in your mind, but for now we will practice by writing them all out.

PREP TOOL #1: BUBBLES & VENN

This step is meant to help you make connections between the things you have read. It should also help you to start analyzing what you have read so that you can start forming your own ideas. For this step, you have the choice of two processes. The first is commonly called a Venn diagram, and the second is what I call Bubbles.

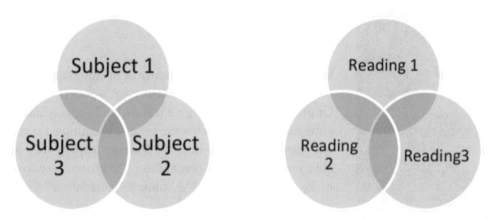

You can use a Venn diagram, like the examples here, to compare ideas and readings. In the first image, you would put into each circle the unique points about a certain idea. In the parts where they intersect, you would jot down the things they have in common. Notice that Subject 1 and Subject 2 may have things in common, which Subject 3 does not, and likewise Subjects 1 and 3, and 2 and 3 may have things uniquely in common. Hopefully you can see how this might be extremely useful for analyzing readings. Most instructors want you to extrapolate what is important from readings on your own, and will probably do a giddy happy-dance if you can also extrapolate how the ideas from different readings are related to each other. Another way you can do this same thing is to use what I call Bubbles. As you see below, in the Bubbles paradigm, you write into each Bubble the important points or ideas of a reading. Then, you draw lines between the bubbles that are related to each other. It is important to note that you should be writing what the relationship *is* on the line, so that you will remember later. Also note that a relationship does not necessarily mean that the two points have to be similar. Relationships could include being the exact opposites, or a cause-and-effect relationship. In essence, play Connect the Dots!

Best practice with these types of exercises is to hand draw and write everything. However, if you feel that you need to use a ready-made worksheet, you can find them in the back of the book.

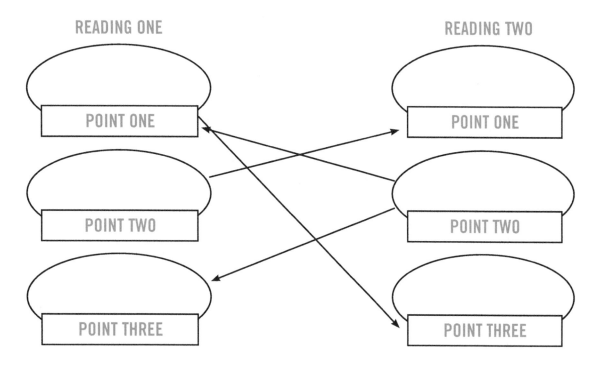

PREP TOOL #2: CONCEPT MAP

Have you ever been told that your memory is like a giant filing cabinet, everything in its own folder, cross referenced with other things similar to it? This is a popular analogy that is totally wrong! Your mind and your memory are nowhere near as nice and orderly as a filing cabinet. Your mind is extremely messy, but that messiness is extremely efficient. You are capable of making some amazing connections by intuition, with just a little practice. The way that your brain naturally makes these sorts of associations is in a sort of web, like the one shown here.

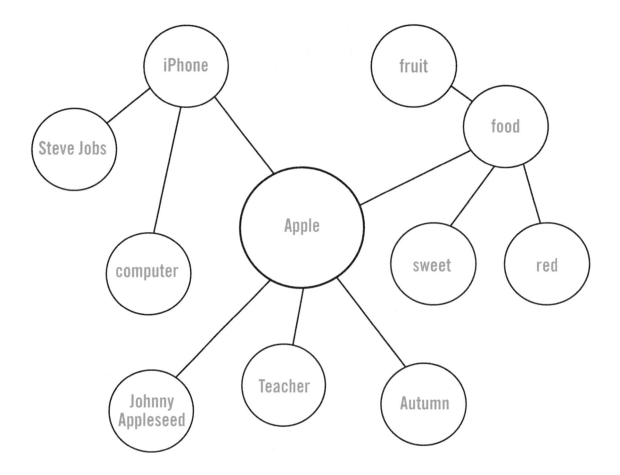

As you can see, everything is linked together by association. Thinking about the word "apple" doesn't automatically lead you to a red, somewhat round fruit. Sometimes it might lead you to a green, somewhat tart fruit, or maybe apple pie, or maybe the computer company "Apple." In reality, you probably think of all of these things all at once, which makes picking them apart somewhat difficult. When you have to pick all of your ideas apart in order to single out just one, or even just a few, in order to write about them, drawing a concept map similar to this can be extremely useful. It allows you to follow the path your brain is taking naturally, but it also allows you to begin grouping ideas in a way that you can later turn into an outline. Fill in the example provided.

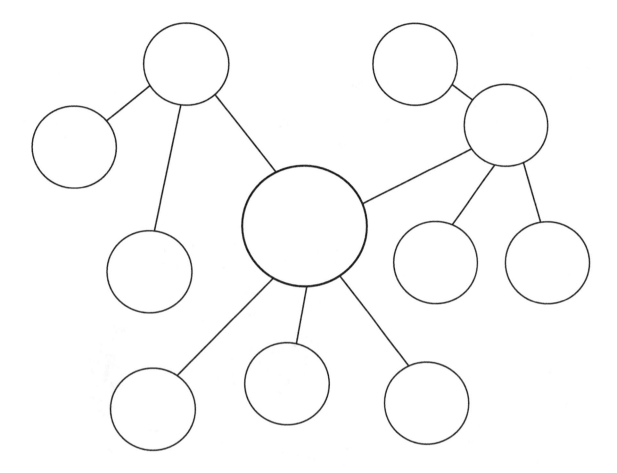

Now, box in the four essay ideas you have come up with. Did you find them? Each secondary circle, surrounded by three smaller circles, is an idea for an essay topic, complete with three main points. A fourth idea would be to use your main center circle as your essay topic with your secondary circles as your main points, which then would each have three details. Which set you go with might depend on the length of your essay, or the assignment requirements that your instructor has given you. No matter what, you should now have at least four options for writing your essay!

Note here that best practice when coming up with your own concept map is to aim for the 3 by 3 rule: for each circle, have at least 3 tertiary circles so that, in all, you have drawn 13 circles. If you cannot come up with at least 3 points for each topic, it may not work as a topic for an essay. That is not a hard-fast rule, though, so it is always best to simply draw a concept map by hand. Many computer programs, such as Microsoft Word, also have functions that will allow you to create a concept map.

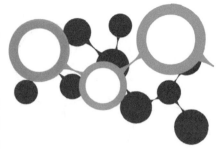

JOURNAL 2

Write one page about why you are in college.
Be honest! Is it because your parents said you had to? Because you didn't know what else to do? Because you know you need a degree to get a good job? What is it that motivates you to be here?

PREP TOOL #3: OUTLINES

You were probably asked to do outlines in high school, or maybe even in junior high. Someone may have gone through with you what an outline looks like, and explained to you that outlines are used to help you write your essays. You may even have been shown an example, but commonly that is as far as instruction in outlining goes. Many students say that they usually write their outline after they've written their paper, just to fulfill the requirement, which completely defeats the point!

"When you put it like that, it makes complete sense."

© Cartoonresource/Shutterstock.com

How do you think you can sit down and write an essay without any stress, and still get an A? The answer is an outline. If done properly, an outline will mean that you will never again open a blank Word document and immediately think to yourself, "I don't know where to start," or end up with an essay that skips and jumps all over the place without having a real point. In GPS terms, and outline is your automated little voice saying, "Turn left in one mile" and "Updating."

The only way an outline is useful is if you do it correctly. So, first things first: let's start with formatting.

I. Subject (Intro)
  A.
  B.
  C.
II. Subject (Main Point 1)
  A.
    1.
  B.
    1.
III. Subject
  A. Topic
    1. Detail
      a. Support
        i. Support
    2. Detail
      a. Support
        i. Support
      b. Support
        i. Support
        ii. Support
  B. Topic

As you can see, outlines operate in a repeating pattern. The large Roman numeral labels the section of the essay, the large Arabic letter labels the topics for each section, and the small Arabic letters and Roman numerals allow you to add detail and support. This allows you to assign a specific place for each piece of information, determining which pieces of information should go together and in what order. This is how you will transform the ideas you came up with in your concept map into a more organized pattern that another person will be able to follow. When you turn in an outline, you should use this format.

This is all well and good, but if you don't fill out the outline properly, it doesn't help much. Many people think that you need only put a word or two next to each symbol, but how does that help you when you pull out your computer to write? If you still have to think about what to write when you sit down to do it, you haven't done your prep work properly. Instead, you should use full phrases and citations in your outline so that when you sit down to write, all you really need to do is translate your outline into sentences and paragraphs. (As you get into your final years of university and have to start writing far longer essays, your outline will not reflect your essay sentence by sentence, but for very short essays you can do a detailed outline.) Consider the following example.

Intro
    A. Hook/Bait – Strawberry i.c. most pop flavor since 1912 (source)
    B. Background – when straw first available, how many brands now
    C. Thesis – "Strawberry ice cream is the best kind of ice cream because it has unique texture, rich flavor, and is a classic option."
II. Texture
    A. Straw ic has unique texture b/c of the chunks
        1. Started having chunks in 1920
    B. Was first i.c. to have pieces in it
        1. Now it's really popular
            a. All kinds of ic has candy, cookies, etc in it
III. Flavor
    A. Has rich flavor cause of percentage of fruit
        1. (source) about how much fruit
        2. Quote – Name, pg #
    B.
IV. Classic Option
    A. Staw ic been available since vanilla & choc
    B. Considered most classic, next to van & choc

You can see that these phrases and notes should be easy to convert into proper sentences. There is enough here to fill out at least one complex sentence, or perhaps even two sentences, for each point. You could probably sit down right now and start to type out this essay without having much else to help you because it is basically already written. This is how an outline should function—a template so detailed that you do not have to do any real thinking in the process of writing out the words. This should leave your mind the room to pay more attention to grammar and punctuation so that later, in a second draft, you have fewer mistakes to change. So outlines actually save you a lot of time and effort!!

Now, there are two basic types of outlines: alternating and block. In an alternating outline, you write about your subjects one after another under each topic so as to show how they both fit under that topic. In a block outline, you write all about one subject and then you write all about another. For example, in an essay comparing two universities, you might look at such topics as academics, cost, and activities.

Alternating	Block
I. Intro	I. Intro
II. Academics	II. University 1
A. University 1	A. Academics
B. University 2	B. Cost
III. Cost	C. Activities
A. University 1	III. University 2
B. University 2	A. Academics
IV. Activities	B. Cost
A. University 1	C. Activities
B. University 2	IV. Conclusion
IV. Conclusion	

Both types of outlines have their uses and their drawbacks. It is up to you to decide which will work best for the essay you are writing. There are times, however, when the essay will seem to "choose" for you; for example, in the essay about strawberry ice cream, it would have been very difficult to format that into a block outline. The topic called for an alternating outline.

To review: there are five steps to prep. The first is simply to read and annotate whatever materials you might be given or might have found during research. After that, the following steps should be done on paper:

1. Venn or Bubbles
2. Concept Map
3. Thesis Sentence
4. Outline

Introduction to Grammar

How do you expect others to understand your point if you aren't writing sentences that they understand? Remember, the brain processes written and verbal language differently, so even if you have written a sentence the way you would say it, expecting that someone else will understand it simply because they would if they heard it, doesn't mean their brain will be able to make that leap to understanding when they read it. We may not like it, but grammar really is an important aspect of writing. While it's true that we all speak English every day, we do so with our own little differences. The small differences in how we structure sentences and the words we use, even how we pronounce them, can affect the meaning of what we say. Common English grammar rules mean that no matter where we are from, as long as we can read English, we will understand what has been written. Remember first things first: You have to be able to write a sentence before you can write an entire essay!

Grammar Lesson #1: Run-ons and Comma Splices

Run-ons (ROs) and comma splices (CSs) are two of the easiest mistakes to fix once you know what to look for. Essentially, they are simple punctuation mistakes, which means that oftentimes you can correct them with a change in punctuation. This isn't always true, so you will need to pay attention to each specific case to determine what changes need to be made.

A run-on sentence occurs when you have combined two or more complete thoughts without proper punctuation between them. If the two segments of a sentence are complete thoughts (and can stand without the other), they should be separated either by a period or a semicolon. Sometimes there are extraneous words in between the segments that will need to be removed or replaced.

A comma splice occurs when you have combined two complete sentences improperly with a comma (rather than a period or semicolon). Obviously, the easiest fix is simply to replace the comma with a period or semicolon and change the capitalization to match. You may occasionally also have to add, replace, or change wording.

GRAMMAR WORKSHEET #1

Name:_____

PRACTICE EXERCISE #1

Directions: Label each sentences as RO (run-on sentence) or C (correct). For any sentences labeled RO, correct them.

Practice: Tommy loved writing music for his band he hated writing papers for school.
RO: Tommy loved writing music for his band**, yet** he hated writing papers for school.

_____ 1. In the morning, I brush my teeth I make sure to grab a large cup of coffee.

_____

_____ 2. After I leave work, I drive home and make my family dinner.

_____

_____ 3. If the bus is late this morning, I will receive another tardy, I hope it's on time.

_____

_____ 4. Jimmy won first place for his science project, Sue was upset by the results.

_____

_____ 5. After the girls practiced for the big game, they relaxed and went to the mall.

_____

From *Maps for Grammar & Writing* by Cindy Beck, Jason Hancock, & Jessica Wise. Copyright © 2012 by Kendall Hunt Publishing Company.

PRACTICE EXERCISE #2

Directions: Read the paragraph and circle any run-on errors. Make sure to also correct those errors.

Potty Training for Fido

Last week, our mom let us purchase our first pet, it was a Golden Retriever. We named him "Fido," and I knew the two of us would be the best of friends. The rule was my sister and I had to be the ones to walk him, bathe him, feed him and train him, this has turned out to be more responsibility than either of imagined. First, he splashes water out of the tub during bath time, creating an even bigger mess. Then, when it's time to walk him, he cries on the leash he would rather run freely. Next, feeding time is pretty easy because Fido already knows that we will put treats in with his food. As soon as he finishes his meal, he has to go to the bathroom, we waited too long several times, our mom was really upset. Therefore, we take Fido out as soon as he walks away from his dog bowl. Finally, training him to go potty outside has been a real challenge he would rather just play outside. In the end, my sister and I are both very happy that we talked our mom into buying us a dog, this great level of responsibility will really help us in the long run. Besides, Fido is already turning out to be the best buddy.

LESSON THREE

Peer Editing

If you have ever taken an English or writing class before, then you have probably been asked to peer edit before. This process usually involves you trading work with a classmate and then each of you trying to find as many mistakes in the other person's work as you can. Now, let's be honest, you probably didn't do a great job and the notes you got back from your classmate probably didn't help you much either. Too often, students aren't actually trained in how to do a peer edit properly, which leaves the exercise essentially pointless.

For every essay assignment, you will be required to bring an extra copy of your rough draft to class to trade with a classmate to do a peer edit. Why? How does peer editing actually help you? After all, aren't your fellow classmates at the same level as you are, making the same kinds of mistakes? Isn't it much more useful to you for your instructor to look over your rough draft? Sure, if you're just looking for someone else to point out all of your mistakes, that's your best bet. Doing a peer edit, however, is beneficial in many other ways.

First, you get another set of eyes on your work. Your brain is designed to spell and grammar check for you. It will actually correct mistakes as you read so that the mistakes don't trip you up. This means that you literally can't see your mistakes! Because your brain knows what you *meant* to write, it fixes the problem for you in your mind so you don't notice it. When another person read your work, they will catch those mistakes, things like misspellings or typos, which your brain auto-corrected.

Therefore, it is important to do peer edits in order to help train your brain to catch mistakes when you read. Looking at a classmate's work will allow your brain to form the synaptic pathways for catching written mistakes, which it can then utilize later when you look at your own work. This could take some time, so practice is important. And unfortunately, there is a downside: Once you've taught your brain to catch those mistakes, it always will. You may find yourself picking mistakes out of newspaper, magazine, and internet articles for the rest of your life. Sorry!

Secondly, you will get valuable input from another source about whether or not your essay makes sense and contains all of the information you needed to include. If your classmate returns your essay with a note that says, "I'm not really sure what you were trying to argue," then you know you didn't explain your argument very well. If you get a note back that says, "I see what you were trying to say, but I still disagree," then you might want to look at whether or not you provided enough fac-tual evidence. You could also get comments back about technical aspects of writing. For example, "You use the word 'next' too often" or "Your sentences are really long and get confusing." These are all very helpful notes to have!

Now that you understand why you are being asked to do a peer edit, and how it's supposed to help, let's do some practice together. Here is a student's first draft of a summary essay. Follow the directions on the worksheet to complete a peer edit. We will review this work in class.

Name of Editor: _____ Name of Author: _____

Essay # _____ Essay Type: _____

Directions:
1. Identify the topic/thesis statement.
2. Identify punctuation and grammar mistakes on your partner's essay.
3. Identify any awkward or wordy sentences. Attempt to rewrite a few so that they work better.
4. Write a note on content: Does it flow/have logic? Does it meet requirements?

1. Thesis Statement: _____

_____

_____

2. Grammatical Mistakes: Make marks and/or notations within the text.

3. Style: Rewrite sentences here.

_____

_____

_____

_____

_____

_____

_____

_____

_____

4. Note on Content: _____

_____

_____

_____

_____

_____

_____

_____

English 101

March 1, 2010

A New Take on Food- Summary of *In Defense of Food*

Michael Pollan, author of The Omnivores' Dilemma, continues his journalistic career in his next book titled *In the Defense of Food*. Here he talks more about what foods should be eaten and the background of how our culture's mind set on food has developed. He starts off with some basic background information to help set up the story and then moves into what he will talk about in the different sections of the book.

Pollan starts off by simply stating that humans should just eat food. This includes lots of plants and some meat, in a balanced way to help promote good health. Pollan then talks about the difference between food and processed food. Processed food comes with health claims and that means that it is only editable, not necessary food or good for a person to eat. These are the foods that people should stay the hell away from, buy fresh food nothing with health claims. Next, Pollan raises the question as to why humans now, of all times, need to ask people what to eat? He answers this question in more detail later in the book with more complex examples and whys but now simply states that it is a change in culture using a story he explains that his mother's mother –back in the 1960's- did all the cooking from scratch, basically making up the recipe from start. Over time these kinds of methods disappeared because of science. Science became the lader in food marketing and processing and made its way into the homes of everyone that cooked. Usually starting with the daughters of the home because the daughters was an easier target to attract. Pollan than starts to state the main reasons as to why the food companies moved from trying to attract the mothers to the daughters. After that Pollan then states two studies –of 2005 and 2006 - that refute earlier statements that attracted their new target audience to the new foods that were unquestionably the best foods to hit the market of the time. He makes this point to prepare the reader for what he will explain later on in the book, this is to show how everything up to this point has been nothing but a marketing scheme to make money and not necessary benefit people's health.

Next Pollen moves into what the actual book is going to be about. Pollen recaps that what most people eat today is not exactly what he would call food. It is a processed, edible, food like substance, nor is the way we eat the food exactly healthy either. Further explaining that it is scientists that have got people to believe that the food is not important but what the food contains. Pollen explains that eating is more then just for survival it is about pleasure, family and finding's one self. That eating is about the culture in which someone lives. Pollen conveys that he does not want for people to stop caring about their health or what they eat for the American diet has it's own issues. Pollan's final goal of this book is to set up eating guidelines, something that he will cover in the final section.

Name:_____

Grammar Lesson 2: Fragments

As the label indicates, fragments (FRGs) are pieces of sentences. They are either phrases that make no sense on their own, or they are dependent phrases that you can maybe figure out, but rely on other information or other sentences in order to really make sense. (The problem with this second type of fragment is that not everyone will make the correct association.)

There are three elements of a sentence:

Subject (who or what)   Verb (doing)   Complete Thought

If the particular bit of language you are considering is missing any of these three things, it is not a sentence (and is therefore a fragment). Fragments can often easily be fixed by adding a subject or verb. If the element of complete thought is missing, though, you may have to do some rewording in order to repair the fragment.

PRACTICE EXERCISE #1

Directions: Identify which element is missing, then rewrite the sentence correctly.

1. After you finish the dishes. _____

_____

2. Because the river flooded. _____

_____

3. Until the owner decided to close the restaurant. _____

_____

From *Maps for Grammar & Writing* by Cindy Beck, Jason Hancock, & Jessica Wise. Copyright © 2012 by Kendall Hunt Publishing Company.

4. Whenever you get home. _____

_____

5. Unless you plan on getting a job. _____

_____

PRACTICE EXERCISE #2

Directions: Indicate whether each the following groups of words is a sentence fragment (FRG) or complete thought (C).

1. The lock on the back door had been pried open. _____
2. As a former basketball and football player. _____
3. Although Jayla has all of her nursing prerequisites. _____
4. Running through the halls yelling Brandon's name. _____
5. Although he had trained all year, Axel could not finish the race. _____
6. Jay Leno, a popular late night television host. _____
7. Cameron unwilling to give Ana Sofia the respect she deserves. _____
8. Malik will not go to the movie unless you will pay his way. _____
9. Emily forgot to let Carson know where the dance is being held. _____
10. Trying not to laugh, Madison answered the phone. _____

Essay Mode—Compare and Contrast

Throughout your academic career, you will be continually asked to read this and that in various classes. Sometimes your professor will guide you through the connections between the things you read and the concepts they contain, and other times your professors will expect you to make those connections on your own (which will happen increasingly as you go). You will, hopefully, find as you take more and more classes that you are making connections between something you heard or read in one class and what you are studying in another class. Even better, you may find yourself starting to make connections between the things you are learning about in school and the things going on around you in the world, particularly the things you see, read, or hear about in media.

You may not have a whole lot of practice in doing this yet, though. This is another one of those skills that will develop only through constant practice. Eventually, you will have trained your brain to make connections without thinking too hard about it, but until those neural networks are established, you're going to have to put some conscious effort into drawing out those connections. A compare/contrast essay can help you start to establish this new skill.

You may have written a compare/contrast essay previously, either in high school or elementary school. There is quite a difference, though, between writing about how one article is similar or different from another article and writing about the similarities and differences between **abstract concepts** (or between ideas which don't seem to be related). This assignment requires you to think a little bit beyond what first comes to mind. You will be showing that you are capable of thinking beyond the information that is presented in an article and are able to link ideas in one article to ideas in another.

NOTE ·

Abstract means something you can't physically touch. You can touch your desk, for example; it is in no way abstract. It has definable dimensions, like height, weight, width, et cetera. You can feel the air, but it is a little less substantial. It has some definable dimensions, like temperature, but it is harder to describe. Abstract means you can't touch it at all—there are no definable dimensions. A concept is a synonym for an idea. Put the two words together and you get an idea that is difficult to define.

Let's try this out together. For this assignment, you should be making good use of the Venn diagram and Bubbles worksheets we learned about in the Steps to Prep section. Fill out the Venn diagram, putting the term "Learning" on one side and the term "Education" on the other side. Make sure you're thinking carefully about how "learning" might be different from "education," as well as about what they have in common!

Notice how the things you are comparing/contrasting here are not articles? They are concepts, ideas. Most professors will be far more impressed (and give higher grades) with an essay that looks beyond the surface. If they wanted to know what one article says versus what another article says, they can (and probably have) read it themselves! So, for this essay, do NOT simply compare two things you have read. Look at the ideas, and try to draw together thoughts about how or why the connections exist.

Lucky you! I've picked a topic for this essay, which is cultural differences. A culture is a group of people who share habits of dress, language, eating, moral or ethical codes, music, a common history, and *sometimes* religion, government, or geographical location. Examples include the French people (dress, language, food/eating, ethical codes, geographical location, and government), Jewish people (dress, language, food/eating, religion), and people from the Middle East (dress, language, food/eating). There are also subcultures within dominant cultures. An example of this might include African American culture within American culture.

Compare/Contrast

GOALS:

> Demonstrate a sense of critical thinking and thesis
> Demonstrate an ability to identify and display pertinent information
> Demonstrate a sense of organization
> Demonstrate a collegiate level of writing (sentence structure, punctuation, etc.)

DIRECTIONS:

Compare _and_ contrast the practices of another culture with those of Americans. Essentially, demonstrate how the two cultures do things similarly and differently. Try to extend beyond literal behavioral practices and discuss influences for those practices, which means you may need to make educated guesses about why a particular culture does one thing one way versus why the other culture does it a different way, or why they both do things similarly. You **MUST** find at least one source that describes the practices of the "other" culture you choose. (See Choices, next.) Attempt to remain unbiased: Do not refer to Americans as "we" or "us," for example, and avoid using language that would indicate one way of doing something is better than the other. (Also, there should be no use of first-person pronouns such as "I" or "me.")

CHOICES:

You may choose any other culture to compare Americans to. You may wish to choose another culture that you are somewhat familiar with. You may use one of the following areas to help you determine which practices to compare and contrast:

- Education
- Food/eating
- Family life

You will need to find at least one source that describes the practices in the country you choose. You may ask for help at the library, or you may visit your professor during office hours for help. Here are some other suggestions:

- Google Scholar: www.googlescholar.com
- Library databases
- Online encyclopedias: www.britannica.com, www.worldbook.com

I **do not** recommend searching with a browser like Yahoo! or Bing. **You may not use Wikipedia.**

REQUIREMENTS:

- _____ words
- Two lines of direct quote (no more)
- A page listing the sources you use (bibliography or works cited page)
- Staple prep work to the back of the rough draft
- Proper formatting (per syllabus)

PRACTICE: STUDENT ESSAY #2

Name:_____

Following is the student example of a compare/contrast essay to help you understand what you should be doing. Keep in mind that this is a real example, and so it is not "perfect." Follow the directions to help you analyze the example.

Directions: After reading and annotating the article, complete the worksheet. Detach all of the work from your book, staple together with this worksheet on top, and bring to class.

In yellow, highlight the thesis statement.
In pink, highlight each topic sentence or main point.
In blue, highlight the summarizing or comparison words and phrases.
In green, highlight any vocabulary you are unfamiliar with.
Circle with a pen any grammatical or punctuation mistakes you find.

Answer the following:

1. Identify what this essay is comparing. _____

   _____

2. Who do you think is the audience for this essay? _____

   _____

3. What do you think is the purpose of this essay? _____

   _____

4. Do you think this essay achieves the goals of a comparison? How? _____

   _____

Mike Kruger

September 23, 2015

448 Words

Santa or Sankt Nikolaus? Stockings or shoes? Many American Christmas traditions are originally from Germany, but there are still many differences today. The general ideas of Christmas itself were carried over from Germany and other European countries. For example, "the Christmas tree custom was brought to the US by German immigrants" (German way). Many U.S traditions have evolved from old traditions to adapt to our society. German and U.S culture have some similarities when it comes to Christmas traditions, but are different in a lot of ways.

Santa and Sankt Nikolaus are two entirely different (fictional) people. Santa is the U.S version of Sankt Nikolaus who was created in the early 1900's for children. The German version Sankt Nikolaus was believed to be an actual person who lived long ago. The German Sankt Nikolaus does not have elves like the American Santa does; instead he has "krampusse", which are small creatures that help him with the gifts. While both elves and krampusse both give out gifts to children, krampusse are considered to be devilishly looking with horns, as opposed to friendly little elves.

Christmas day in Germany is very different than Christmas day in the U.S. In Germany Christmas day and Christmas Eve have no relation to any Santa type figure. For most parts of Germany, the day is strictly religious. Most of Germany celebrates Sankt Nikolaus day, which is on December 6. The U.S combines the religious part with the Santa part for Christmas day. The biggest similarity is that there is still gift giving for both cultures on Christmas day.

Christmas trees were a tradition originally from Germany. While both countries use Christmas trees, there are some differences. While more Americans have started to switch over to fake trees for their benefits, in Germany it is custom to have a real fir tree. Germans also traditionally use real candles for the light on their tree, while Americans use small glass lights that they wrap around the tree. The tradition of hanging glass ornaments on the tree is also from Germany. Both the U.S and Germany use glass ornaments, but in German culture the ornaments usually have more meaning.

It makes sense that German culture and American culture share many similarities about Christmas because the German people originally brought the traditions over. There are less similarities today but still both cultures use trees, wish lists, and chocolate filled advent calendars. Some of the original traditions have faded out through the years but still the connection can be made. German and U.S culture have some similarities when it comes to Christmas traditions, but are very different in a lot of ways.

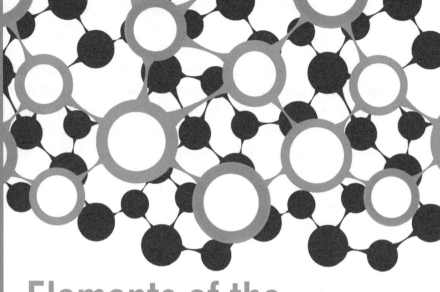

LESSON FOUR

Elements of the Essay: Introductions

Every essay has to start somewhere. A blank page can be pretty daunting, but if you've done your prep work, you shouldn't have any problem knowing where to start. From your outline, you already know what information you're going to start with, but there is more to the beginning of an essay than just slapping three or four sentences together!

The introduction to your essay is just as important as the body of the essay. The introduction is what gets your reader familiar with your topic, your tone, and the purpose of your essay. Think about our GPS analogy. If you were to start with your first direction, "Turn left on Broad Street," you may feel a little lost right from the start. Where are you turning left onto Broad Street from? What is your final destination? Are you taking the shortest distance route, or the shortest time route? These are the kind of questions you don't want your readers to be asking. A good introduction will give them all of that information.

> **NOTE** ·
>
> The introduction is part of a repetition pattern. Humans remember information best when it has been presented multiple times. The repetition pattern for an essay basically requires that you first "Tell me what you are going to tell me," then "Tell me," and finally "Tell me what you just told me." It may seem a little ridiculous, and redundant, but you will find that it is very effective!

There are three elements of a good introduction:
1. Hook or Bait
2. Background
3. Thesis Statement

Intro Tool #1: Hook/Bait

If you were going fishing, you wouldn't throw a line into the water without anything on the end, would you? You need bait to draw the fish to you, and then a hook to catch them with, right? The first line of your essay should serve the same function. First, you want to draw your readers' interest, and then you want to catch their attention. There are a myriad of ways you can do that, but these are the traditional options.

1. Quote: _____

   _____

2. Question: _____

   _____

3. Shocking Fact: _____

   _____

4. Allusion: _____

_____

Intro Tool #2: Background

It is easy to think that, because you are familiar with a topic, your readers must be as well. However, you should assume that your readers live in a vacuum—that is, that they have no prior knowledge of your topic or anything associated with it. The few lines in your introduction between your hook and your thesis statement should be used to bring your readers "up to speed" on whatever information is most important to your topic.

For example, if I were going to be writing an essay arguing for the use of body cameras by police officers, I might write a few sentences outlining the recent media obsession and cultural attention on police brutality. Saying that it has been a topic of interest in our country does not indicate anything about my assertion nor about the reasons why I think body cameras should be used; it simply lets the readers know why I'm writing about it. The information you provide in the background section of your introduction will vary depending on the topic you are writing about and what mode of essay you are writing. So, if you are writing a critique, for example, you would use this space to tell about the article you are critiquing and its author.

It can be tricky to figure out what to include in this section. Just remember that this part of your essay is called an Introduction, and its purpose is to *introduce* your topic. Let's do some practice.

PRACTICE EXERCISE #1: BACKGROUND

Let's say that you are going to write an essay about your favorite song, book, or movie. First, write two sentences of background for an essay of critique.

_____

_____

_____

_____

Now let's say that you are going to be writing an essay of analysis, and your topic is regarding how this song/book/movie fits into the current popular trend in American culture. Write three sentences of background for that essay.

_____

_____

_____

_____

_____

What was the difference between the two essays? Why do you think you included different information in the second than you did in the first?

_____

_____

_____

_____

_____

Intro Tool #3: Thesis Statements

Think about how you would go about figuring out how to get someplace you've never been before. Most likely, you would enter the new address in your phone or other device and allow GPS to tell you how to get there. If you are like me, you like having the turn-by-turn directions. A thesis statement in an essay operates somewhat like GPS on your phone; it should be telling you exactly what points you are going to make, as well as what destination you are trying to reach.

The "destination" of your thesis statement is called an **assertion**. An assertion is the main point, goal, or aim of your essay. In an argumentative essay, it is the thing you are trying to convince your readers of. In a comparison essay, it is the determination of how two things are either similar, dissimilar, or a little of both. You can usually identify an assertion with words such as:

is (not)	should (not)	are (not)	could (not)
can (not)	would (not)	will (not)	

For example: "Strawberry ice cream _is_ the best kind of ice cream." This sentence tells me what the aim or main point of the essay is; to convince the reader that strawberry ice cream is better than all other kinds of ice cream.

GPS isn't much good, though, if it only tells you where you are going, and not how you are going to get there. Therefore, a thesis statement also needs to reveal the main points of support. The main points of support are those things that will prove or explain the assertion. They often answer the question of "why?" or sometimes "how?"

For example: "Strawberry ice cream is the best kind of ice cream because it has unique texture, rich flavor, and is a classic option." The three answers to "why is strawberry ice cream the best?" are, according to this essay, that it has unique texture, rich flavor, and is a classic option. The task of the body of the essay, then, is to give enough detail about these points so as to convince the reader that they support the assertion, but at least we know what streets we will be turning down!

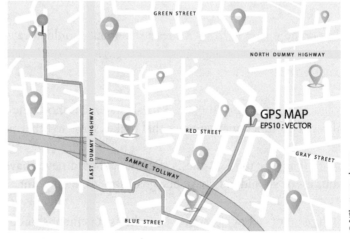

There is a formula for writing a thesis statement, and in foundation level composition courses it will help you to learn what should be included in a thesis statement. It is very important to note, however, that once you have "mastered" the concept, _it is important to break out of the formulaic thesis statement because most instructors, whether in English classes or other classes, do not like them_. In addition, a formulaic thesis statement really only works for essays between two and five pages in length; anything less than two pages would require a much simpler thesis, and anything much longer than five pages would require a much more complex thesis statement. Yet, it is important to learn a rule before you go around bending or breaking it, so let's look at the formula.

Assertion + Main Point 1 + Main Point 2 + Main Point 3 = Thesis

You can see that this formula gives a "destination" for your essay (assertion) and gives the "turn by turn directions" (the main points you will expand upon). Our strawberry ice cream example follows this formula well.

Strawberry ice cream _is_ the best kind of ice cream because it has a unique texture, rich flavor, and is a classic option.

MP3   Assertion   plus sign   MP1   MP2

(+)

• A thesis sentence should always be a complete and correct sentence! •

Following the formula and knowing what pieces of information should be in a thesis statement should keep you on track, but it is easy to get derailed and end up with a thesis statement that doesn't work. The following are some examples of common mistakes, so you can avoid them.

Too broad or too narrow: A thesis statement should always fit the essay you are writing! Don't try to cover a lot of information in a short essay, and don't focus on something too specific to fill your page length!

Vague, unclear, or incomplete: A thesis statement should never be just a phrase (like a title). It should always be a functional sentence that makes sense to other people, and it should always be specific.

More than one topic: A thesis statement should never have more than one assertion! Remember, your essay should only have one goal, aim, or main point.

Statement of fact or observation: A thesis statement should never be inarguable. A reasonable person should always be able to counter your thesis in some way.

An announcement: You should not refer to your essay in your essay. Therefore, a thesis statement should never include wording such as "In this essay" or "The thesis of this paper is...." Unless otherwise told by your instructor, you should also never use "I think" or "In my opinion."

We know that practice is what will actually help you learn, so let's do some practice with thesis statements. Rewrite the following into proper thesis statements.

1. The movie *The Avengers* came out in 2012. _____

_____

2. Good Marvel Movies. _____

_____

3. All of the superhero movies have had an important impact on our society. _____

_____

4. They were successful because of *Iron Man*, *Iron Man 2*, and *Iron Man 3*. _____

_____

5. In this essay, I will discuss the significance of the character of The Black Widow, played by Scarlett Johanssen, throughout the Marvel Avengers movies. _____

_____

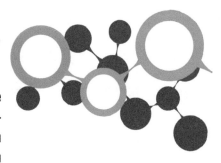

JOURNAL 3

What are the benefits of going to college? Think beyond the standard "getting a good job." First, what about going to college helps you get that job? What other benefits are there in a shaky economy where a college degree doesn't guarantee a good job?

GRAMMAR WORKSHEET #3

Name:_____

Grammar Lesson 3: Parallelism

A sentence should always agree with itself. In fact, a sentence should usually agree with the sentences around it, too. That goes not only for the content of the sentence (you don't want to contradict yourself!) but also for the grammar of the sentence. Sometimes, when we speak, we don't always use the same tense or endings sentence to sentence, or even within sentences. While the part of your brain that translates heard language is pretty good at figuring that all out, the part of your brain that translates written language isn't. If your sentences don't agree with themselves, your reader will get confused, perhaps have to reread several times, and end up feeling like they lost the train of thought. Your sentences should be parallel, or consistent, with themselves and each other.

PRACTICE EXERCISE #2

Directions: Rewrite the sentences correctly.

1. Tomorrow, I will be going to class, taking my test, and tell the professor I leave for break early.

    _____

2. My friends and I have gotten tickets to the new superhero movie, got passes for the after party, and received coupons for free popcorn and soda! _____

    _____

3. To eat out is always fun, and eating exotic cuisine is my favorite thing to be doing. _____

    _____

Directions: Edit the paragraph, correcting any faulty parallelism.

My Saturday is usually busy. I first wake up and go running. After running, I enjoy eating breakfast, resting, and I sit on the front porch for a while. After resting for a bit, I decide to take a bath, relaxing in the tub. When I finish taking a bath, I get dressed and to start a load of laundry. When doing my laundry, the most important steps are sorting, washing, and to fold the clothes afterwards. I hate to fold close and putting them away. Even though I hate doing it, it must be done. After the clothes are finished, I always go to the store to pick up groceries. The grocery store is a great getaway for me. The employees help nicely, courteously, and in a calm manner. I also go visit my grandmother sometimes when I finish getting groceries. I don't get to visit often, so I try to go and visit when I can. Afterwards, I go straight home, kick off my shoes, getting in more comfortable clothes. That is how my Saturday usually is. I never like to deviate from the norm or starting a new schedule. I love it the way it is.

From *Maps for Grammar & Writing* by Cindy Beck, Jason Hancock, & Jessica Wise. Copyright © 2012 by Kendall Hunt Publishing Company.

ESSAY 3

Essay Mode—Definition

For your third essay assignment, you are being asked to define an abstract concept. This is more difficult than it may sound. In fact, many students say that it the most difficult essay they are asked to write. It will require you to think very hard, and not only hard, but you must also think critically. What does it mean to think "critically"? We already looked at how to do a critique, and both of these aspects of the word lead to the same root, which is skilled or educated judgement. To read critically and to think critically means that you use the knowledge that you have acquired to formulate conclusions or questions about the new information you are acquiring.

The thing that is hard about doing that is no one else can do it for you. There are no guidelines, no "right answer." You cannot Google it, or look it up in any book. Thinking critically means exercising your brain to think beyond the parameters that you've previously established for yourself. For this assignment, you will be asked to define an abstract term. (Remember from our work on the Compare and Contrast Essay what an abstract term is.) This is difficult because, by its very nature, an abstract term doesn't have a perfect definition that everyone agrees on.

So, there are two types of meanings for every word. One, the easy one, is the **denotation**. The denotation is the dictionary definition of a word; that is, it is the definition (or multiple definitions) that everyone agrees on. However, there is another type of meaning for a word, and that is the **connotation**. The connotation is the association of feelings or related ideas that come with every word. For example, when you see the word here, what comes to mind?

Apple

_____

_____

_____

You probably came up with all sorts of things to go with "apple," everything from "eat" and "fruit" to "phone" or "computer." These are all connotative ideas that go with that word. Let's try another one.

Scarlet

_____

_____

_____

How is the word "scarlet" different from the word "red"? What emotions or associations does it arouse that "red" does not? Look at it in a sentence:

She wore a red dress.   She wore a scarlet dress.

What feelings do you get about the scarlet dress versus the red dress? These are the connotations of the word. Everybody has different connotations because they have different experiences with the words or the things the words represent. For example, people who had a lovely childhood in a nice house with both of their parents might have warm, fuzzy feelings when they hear the word "home." However, others who had a difficult childhood, full of poverty and abuse, might have a very negative reaction when they hear the word "home."

PRACTICE EXERCISE #1

Let's try doing an easier, more concrete version of a definition. Here, write as many attributes of the subject as you can think of.

Water

_____   _____

_____   _____

_____   _____

_____   _____

_____   _____

Now, refine that list. Include only the attributes that are *absolutely* required in order for something to be considered water. Think it through carefully. Is ice water? Is juice? Are both oceans and lakes made of the same substance? What about what falls from the sky? How about snow? What if it's only a single drop in the sands of a desert? How about humidity (water in the air)? How are all of these things related?

_____   _____

_____   _____

_____   _____

Your second list was probably much shorter than your first. While water may be many things, there are very limited requirements for something to be defined as water. Now, write out a sentence (or two) that defines water.

_____

_____

PRACTICE EXERCISE #2

Now, most of us will probably agree, for the most part, on what water is and isn't. However, this is an example of the kind of questioning you need to do about your subject in order to do a proper definition of it. Let's try something slightly more difficult, with less definable points.

Color

_____   _____

_____   _____

_____   _____

_____   _____

_____   _____

Now, narrow it down. Remember to only include those elements that are absolutely required. Things to think about include: How would you describe color to a blind person? Does everybody have to see the same thing in order for it to be a color? Is white a color, or is it the absence of color? What about black? How are colors in light different than colors in paint? How do animals and insects perceive color?

_____   _____

_____   _____

_____   _____

Now, write a sentence (or two) that defines color. Try starting with "Color is…."

_____

_____

_____

That was probably a little bit more difficult. Let's up the ante!

Definition

GOALS:

Demonstrate an ability to think critically

Demonstrate an ability to explain abstract ideas in concrete language

Demonstrate a sense of connotation and denotation

Demonstrate a collegiate level of writing (sentence structure, punctuation, etc.)

DIRECTIONS:

Define an abstract term. Be sure to carefully consider and respond to the questions of who, what, where, when, and why, though you should not limit yourself to only answering those questions. Try to think "outside-of-the-box" when considering what *really* defines your topic; what bare minimum requirements would you have to label something as your topic? Consider both your own personal definition as well as a general cultural definition. Think hard about points of view other than your own. The definition should attempt, at least, to be agreeable to everyone in the world. Maintain a formal, academic tone. (You may not use first person.)

TOPICS:

You may choose one of the following terms to define, OR you may choose your own (but that topic MUST be approved by the instructor).

Wealth	**Education**
Sport(s)	**Home**

TIPS:

Make a list of associations you think of when you think of this topic (connotation). What about those associations are unique to you?

Consider how our culture views this term and how people in other cultures view this term.

Determine the minimum requirements for something to be defined as your topic.

REQUIREMENTS:

- _____ words
- Use at least two sources, not including a dictionary
- In-text citations of source(s)
- Use of two quotes, of various lengths

Dear Santa, Just what do you MEAN by naughty?

© debra hughes/Shutterstock.com

Name:_____

Here is the student example of a definition essay to help you understand what you should be doing. Keep in mind that this is a real example, and so it is not "perfect." Follow the directions to help you analyze the example.

DIRECTIONS:

In yellow, highlight the thesis statement.
In pink, highlight each topic sentence or main point.
In blue, highlight the defining words used.
In green, highlight any vocabulary you are unfamiliar with.
Circle with a pen any grammatical or punctuation mistakes you find.

Answer the following:

1. Identify what this essay is defining. _____

_____

2. What criteria did the author use to define this topic? _____

_____

3. Do you think this essay adequately defines the topic? How could the writer have done a better job?

_____

4. Is there a different way of defining this topic? How would you have defined it? _____

_____

Angela Fischer

Due: 10-14-15

Essay 3

Word count: 506

Food

People love to eat and experience the pleasure of food. It sustains us and keeps us alive and healthy. Food is a substance we eat and take into our body that provides nourishment, gives us energy, has taste, and will not be harmful when eaten.

The minute we put food into our mouth, we are nourishing our body. Our body needs food and its nutrients to keep our organs going. The nutrients that make up food are fats, proteins, carbohydrates and amino acids ("Food" <u>Britannica On-line</u>). Each of these elements of food are necessary in a special way and gives us energy. If we as humans did not eat food, we would not thrive. The vitamins and minerals in food also help promote growth and wellbeing ("Nutrition" <u>Britannica On-Line</u>). Food is the key to staying alive.

Since food keeps us alive, it is not going to harm you when you eat it. Food is not going to be poison or toxic. Since it will not harm you, it is edible and can be chewed and swallowed. Rocks and cardboard are examples of something that is not food. A maple leaf cannot be eaten, but a lettuce leaf can. Certain nuts, like almonds, can be eaten, while others, like acorns or buckeyes, cannot because they will cause a human body harm.

In addition to food as a nutrient, food has taste. The taste of food can be flavorful to one person and distasteful to another. Food can be salty, sweet, sour, or a combination of these tastes. Certain food ingredients are found in specific cultural dishes that give them a unique taste. Italian food, for instance, has many dishes made with tomatoes and spices like basil. Mexican food is more on the spicy side, while German food is famous for sausages. Culture has a bearing on the way food looks and tastes based on traditions.

Although the specific taste of food lets us know what we are eating, there are other factors that describe food. Comfort food, when eaten, gives a feeling of warmth and coziness. On a cold winter day, a hot bowl of chicken noodle soup would be comfort food. In an article published in ScienceDaily, our food choices and eating behaviors are affected by social factors. When researching the attraction to comfort food, according to a study done at the University at Buffalo indicated "Because comfort food has a social function, it is especially appealing to us when we are feeling lonely or rejected" (ScienceDaily). Then there is fast food, which a teenager's go-to meal. The quick burger and shake may not be the healthiest, but it is food and nutrition. Home-cooked food and leftovers, like meatloaf for Sunday dinner, have their own meaning to each person and how they grew up.

In conclusion, food is necessary to all living creatures. Culture and traditions can determine the taste and type of food we eat. Food when eaten, gives us the power to survive and grow, and will not hurt us when we digest it.

Work Cited

"Food." *Encyclopedia Britannica. Encyclopedia Britannica Online.* Encyclopedia Britannica Inc. 2015. Web. 11 Oct 2015 http://www.britannica.com/topic/food.

"Nutrition" *Encyclopedia Britannica. Encyclopedia Britannica Online.* Encyclopedia Britannica Inc. 2015. Web. 06 Oct 2015 http://www.britannica.com/topic/food

University of Buffalo. "Love the cook, love the food: Attraction to comfort food linked to positive social connections." ScienceDaily, 27 March 2015. www.sciencedaily.com/releases/2015/03/150327132156.htm.

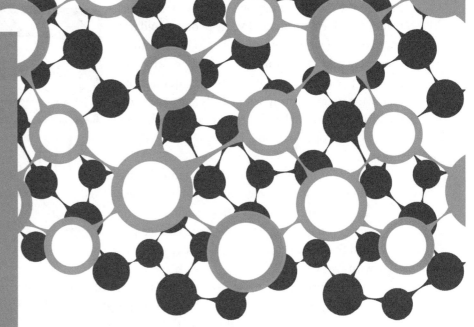

Punctuation

Punctuation seems to be the one thing that most people have a problem with. You learned the basics in elementary school and high school, but somehow you seem to still be making too many mistakes. Honestly, English is a confusing language and the written rules that govern how it works are confusing, too. In the past, when you have had a punctuation question, you may have been directed to a handbook that lists all the different ways various types of punctuation can be used, with examples and exercises to help you understand. The truth is, that probably didn't help you much. What you really need is a concise, easy to understand cheat sheet that will get you through almost any question you have with hundreds of pages to sift through.

Voila!

Back in the day, punctuation marks were symbols readers used to read aloud. (Many people could not read so those who could often read aloud to their friends, family, etc.) So, a comma told you where to pause, a period told you where to end, quotes told you when to use a funny voice. Today, punctuation is a little more formal and is used to create what we refer to as "proper" writing. Here are some helpful hints:

- The period is used to end a statement only when a complete idea has been expressed (or at the end of abbreviations such as Mr. or etc.). Today, it is customary to separate a period from the beginning of the next sentence with two spaces.

! The exclamation mark is used only at the end of a statement where the writer wishes to be especially emphatic (e.g., It was astonishing! **OR** You ugly toad!).

? The question mark is used only at the end of a sentence that is meant to be a question (e.g., Is this a surprise?).

' The apostrophe is used for several purposes:
  - To indicate possession or responsibility (e.g., Krystine's brown hat **OR** The students' home work **OR** Joline's fault)
  - To create contractions: it's (it is), don't (do not), they're (they are), etc.

" " Quotes are used either to indicate a person's speech or to indicate that a word or phrase has not been officially defined in the way the writer is using it (e.g., Krystine's "brown" hat is really gray **OR** The "new" sweater is from Goodwill). Quotes are also used to denote the title of a short work, such as a magazine or a newspaper article.

; The semicolon is used to join two complete, proper sentences that have linked ideas or subjects (e.g., "So, you could replace the semi-colon with a period and each part would still work as two complete but separate sentences; most people use a period instead of a semi-colon.")

: The colon is used to join one complete sentence with a fragment of a sentence that has a relating idea (e.g., "Matt had a large lunch: a banana, two turkey sandwiches, three Twinkies and a Coke.")

, The comma, bain of the English language, is used in several common ways:

1. The comma is most commonly used after the word preceding a linking word such as "or," "but," or "and."
2. The comma is used to separate the items in a list, but not pairs (e.g., The blue, yellow, green, and orange tulips **NOT** The green and blue tulips).
3. The comma is used to separate sections of a sentence called "asides" (e.g., "The duke, <u>a handsome young man,</u> took control of the castle.").
4. The comma is used after quotes (e.g., "You first," Andrew said.).
5. The comma is sometimes used in compound sentences without a linking word (e.g., "She went home, sad and tired.").

Commas are sometimes used in other ways, but these are the most common that you may encounter and/or will use. If you can't decide whether or not you should be using a comma, ask yourself this question: If I were saying this aloud, would I naturally pause or take a breath here? But be careful!! Remember that you must think in terms of Standard American English, not dialect!

<u>**Capital Letters**</u> should begin every new sentence. They are also used with proper nouns such as names of people, places, or significant things (like the Bible).

<u>**Indentations**</u> should be used to begin every new paragraph.

PRACTICE ...

AND THEN PRACTICE MORE

© Cartoonresource/Shutterstock.com

PRACTICE – PUNCTUATION

Name:_____

Directions: Indicate which symbol of punctuation should be used at each point.

[1]In 1977[2] a movie that would become one of the most famous films of all time was released to a small number of theatres in the United States[3] The title of this film was Star Wars[4] [5]a name which is globally recognizable today. The story revolves around several main characters[6] Luke, Leia, Han, Chewie, C-3PO and R2-D2. These characters face a terrible enemy[7] The Emperor and Darth Vader are trying to take over the galaxy[8] Darth Vaders[9] evil plan includes blowing up planets. Its[10] up to Luke and Leia[11] with Han and Chewie[12] to stop him. A critic of the time called the film innovative and stunning.[13](Ebert, 16) *Star Wars* is one of my favorite movies ever[14] What is your favorite movie[15]

1. _____

2. _____

3. _____

4. _____

5. _____

6. _____

7. _____

8. _____

9. _____

10. _____

11. _____

12. _____

13. _____

14. _____

15. _____

Name:_____

Grammar Lesson 4: Commas

In all of writing, comma usage is ranked as the number one mistake. Whether you have used it when you shouldn't have, or haven't used it when you should, commas are tough to figure out. Even professional writers make comma mistakes (fairly often, even) so you shouldn't feel bad about making mistakes with them. This is a tool you are going to have to practice with a lot before you master it!

Use the information about commas found in Lesson Five to complete the following exercises.

PRACTICE EXERCISE #1

Directions: Determine (Y/N) if the **words in bold** need commas between them.

1. _____ I think the decision is up to **you Marcus**.
2. _____ The man who backed into my **car drove** off before I could stop him.
3. _____ They live in a **red brick** house at the end of the street.
4. _____ The restaurant was **crowded but** we were able to get a table quickly.
5. _____ The purpose of the meeting **is to** decide when the next meeting will be.
6. _____ Over the **weekend I** had three animals at my house that did not belong to me: Hickory, Lyra, and Tibby.
7. _____ Many students take classes **online because** of the flexibility.
8. _____ Since his flight was **cancelled he** rented a car and drove to Chicago instead.
9. _____ Hunter is coming home on the **14th which** is my birthday.
10. _____ I always thought it was weird that my mother's **aunt was** married to my father's brother.

From *Maps for Grammar & Writing* by Cindy Beck, Jason Hancock, & Jessica Wise. Copyright © 2012 by Kendall Hunt Publishing Company.

PRACTICE EXERCISE #2

Directions: Read the paragraph and correct any comma errors by adding or omitting commas. Circle your corrections.

Cold and lonely the child ran down the pathways of the city Zoo. It was raining and he lost his mother, while wondering off after she told him to stay close. Nonetheless he was still lost, and was beginning to worry more and more. He turned left down a dark path which led to the alligator pond. The pond was dark and dreary. He remembered seeing it earlier, and started to realize he was going in circles. Out of the corner of his eye he saw the snack stand, that sold lemonade earlier that day. Pacing by the stand his mother was calling his name. He suddenly recognized her and ran into her arms. They immediately headed for the front gate and then to the car to get out of the pouring rain.

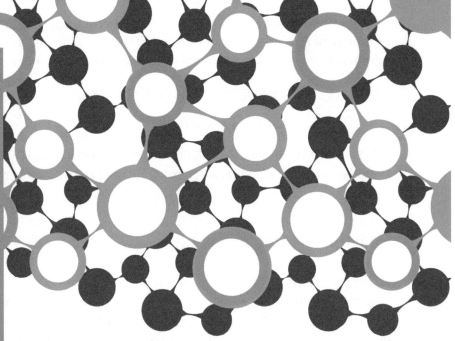

LESSON SIX

Elements of the Essay: Body

In the repetition pattern, the body is the section of your essay where you explain yourself. It is the "Tell Me" section. In this section, all of your main points, ideas, and logic should be explained. This is also where you present all of your evidence: quotes, facts, and other references. Obviously, the body of your essay should constitute the bulk of your work. It should take up about two-thirds of your page length.

Just because the body is considered one section doesn't mean that you should let go of your GPS organization. The body should be divided into sections, too. Traditionally, these sections are divided by topic, or main point. (You should have noticed that fact while doing your outline.) If you have chosen to write an alternating style outline, you will divide your body up into paragraphs that go back and forth, providing the information for one point and then another until all of your points are accounted for. If you have chosen a block style, you will provide all of your information for one point (probably in multiple paragraphs) and then all of the information for your next point until all of your points are accounted for.

NOTE ·

It is important to note that the body of your essay should be made up of several paragraphs, grouped together by point, rather than simply being one or two long paragraphs!

Body Tool #1: Topic Sentence

To help your reader, each time you begin a new point, you should use a **topic sentence**, which is similar to a mini thesis statement for that part of your essay. It should be a complete, correct sentence that gives the readers some idea of which point you are going to be explaining. An easy way to do this is to simply take your assertion from the thesis statement for your essay, and combine it with whichever point you are making. For example:

Thesis Statement for the Essay
↓
Strawberry ice cream is the best kind of ice cream because of its rich texture, deep flavor, and fun color.

Becomes three possible Topic Sentences

Strawberry ice cream is the best because of its rich texture.

Strawberry ice cream is the best because of its deep flavor.

Strawberry ice cream is the best because of its fun color.

From these sentences, you would easily be able to tell what the author is going to explain in that particular section or paragraph of the essay. It is a **signpost statement**: If you have directions on your GPS that tell you to turn left on Main Street, for example, that might be pretty hard to do if the streets aren't labeled! A signpost statement, like a topic sentence, lets your reader know that you are making a turn, that you will now be changing the topic. You may also notice, however, that these sentences are pretty boring, and they are very repetitive. You should try to be creative with your topic sentences, creating signpost statements that aren't so formulaic.

WHAT'S THE POINT?

You may be wondering why all of this is important. Or, maybe you don't really care and are just learning how to do it because you're being told that's how you do it. In order for you to remember all of these tools, though, it is important that you understand *why* they are used. Giving your reader a clear sense of when you are changing topics means that they don't lose any focus on the change; they can easily switch gears, and aren't left wondering, "Wait. How does this information relate to the information I was just reading?" That is important in order to create a sense of cohesion and flow. Now, why is that important? In the end, it means your reader doesn't get to the end of your essay and say, "Wow, that was confusing" and, at least for immediate purposes, that means you end up with a better grade!

PRACTICE EXERCISE #1

Use the following thesis statement to create three distinct topic sentences. Remember, be creative! Don't simply change a few words.

The changing standards of femininity in American Culture are reflected in the increasingly varied roles of female characters in Marvel superhero movies and shows such as The Avengers, Agents of Shield, and Jessica Jones.

1. _____

_____

2. _____

_____

3. _____

_____

Body Tool #2: RENNS

The body of your essay is where you present all of your evidence. You are probably familiar with the term "evidence" from police or detective TV shows and movies. Usually, the evidence is what is gathered by the police and presented in court as "proof" that the person they are blaming is guilty. Without evidence, it's hard to convince a jury, or a judge, that a person should be found guilty of a crime, and in the United States, a person is "presumed innocent until proven otherwise." So, if there is not enough evidence to prove someone is the culprit, the person does not get punished. Evidence in your writing will work similarly; if you don't provide enough of it, your readers will presume you're wrong!

One system of evidence that can be used is known as RENNS. This is a system of types of evidence that can be used to support your points.

R _____

_____

E _____

_____

N _____

_____

N _____

_____

S _____

_____

Name:_____

Grammar Lesson 5: Agreement

Today, using the incorrect pronoun to refer to someone can cause a lot of problems. Our language is still adapting to the new sense of what is discriminatory and what isn't, so replacing a person's name with a pronoun can be tricky and mistakes get made. Some of these mistakes are due to the differences between spoken and written language, which can be more difficult to catch, and others are simply word misuse.

There are two kinds of pronoun errors:
1. Using the incorrect pronoun. A pronoun must match the noun it is replacing in gender and number. Be sure you are using the proper gendered pronoun, but also that if your original noun is singular or plural, the pronoun is as well.
2. Unclarified pronoun. A pronoun must always replace a clarified noun, which means that it should be clear which noun the pronoun is replacing. Unfortunately, when we speak we often use unclarified pronouns, expecting our conversation partner to figure it out from context or to stop us and ask a question. When writing, though, if the noun is not clear, the reader can't simply ask the writer. Keep in mind that a pronoun nearly always will refer to the *immediately preceding* noun, even if it isn't the noun the writer meant for it to replace.

So what do you do if you don't know the gender of the person you want to use a pronoun for? That's still a bit undecided by the experts. The old rule was that if the gender was unknown, you would use the male pronoun, but that's fairly discriminatory. Today, names can still leave you unsure of someone's gender, and if you are referring to a hypothetical person it gets even harder to use an appropriate pronoun.
1. If you can guess the person's gender from the name, you can use that pronoun. If you can't, try using "they" or "their." It is technically incorrect because "they" is plural, but most professors now will accept it.
2. If the person is hypothetical, you can try using "one" or "you" but be careful because repetition of those words can get awkward or confusing.

Still not really sure what to do? The best thing to do is to ask your instructor!

PRACTICE EXERCISE #2

Directions: Circle the correct pronoun.

1. Government workers have to pay (his or her / its / their) taxes just like everyone else.

2. Grandmas and grandpas have it easy; (he or she / they) can spoil (his or her / their) grandkids without dealing with the consequences.

3. The team won (its / their) last five games, and the players were pleased with (its / their) accomplishment.

4. Each father or mother should take responsibility for (his or her / their) children.

5. Showing up late for (your / their / his or her) job could get an employee fired.

PRACTICE EXERCISE #3

Directions: Indicate which pronoun is the problem, the noun it should refer to, and suggest a solution.

Example: Ever since Bill and Jack started dating, his time is pretty limited.
    "his" could refer to either person; Bill's time is limited since he started dating Jack.
    "His" could refer to either person.
    Correction: Bill's time is limited since he started dating Jack.

1. The doctor removed his cast from Jamie's leg, and then he threw it away. _____

    _____

2. Her iPad was in Heather's room, so Taylor texted to ask her to bring it back to her. _____

    _____

3. I wanted to buy a new tablet, but they didn't have one I liked. _____

    _____

4. I sent the enrollment forms for my two children, one of which has been corrected. _____

    _____

From *Maps for Grammar & Writing* by Cindy Beck, Jason Hancock, & Jessica Wise. Copyright © 2012 by Kendall Hunt Publishing Company.

FIRST THINGS FIRST: **Foundational Tools for Collegiate Writing**

5. Lexi and Emma used to be best friends until she started dating Grayson. _____

    _____

6. I wanted to go see the sequel to that movie, but we didn't know it started an hour before we got there.

    _____

7. The professor cancelled class, but they sent their notes and homework assignments anyway.

    _____

Integrating Quotes

How does someone know that the facts you've cited, the experts you've quoted, or the sources you've used are real? After all, wouldn't it be fairly simple to just make all that up? Well, that's why we have academic honesty policies. Now, you should be aware of what **plagiarism** is, and why it's bad. However, a lot of students don't know that incorrectly citing the sources they've used, or not citing them at all, is also plagiarism and violates academic honesty policies.

Up until now, you've probably been doing your best to cite your sources however you learned to do it in high school, and that's fine. Unless you've been told differently by your instructor, you're probably getting a little bit of leeway on this issue because you are in an introductory writing course. After this course is over, though, you will be held accountable for using correct citations, so we better get started on learning them!

Citations Tool #1: In-Text Citations

There are two ways of citing a source in the text of your essay. Some rules and specifications vary depending on what citation style you're using, so you should double check with your instructor about which style is preferred. We'll just learn some *general* ways of citing to keep you out of trouble!

The purpose of a citation is always to lead your readers to your works cited page (or bibliography, depending on style) where they can then go look up the source you used for themselves. There are two ways of citing in your essay.

1. In-Sentence Citations: working the author's name, and possibly the title of the work into a sentence containing a quote or other reference.
2. Parenthetical Citations: contained in parenthesis at the end of a sentence, the author's name, etc.

Incorporating information into a sentence can be a useful way of providing a citation and integrating a quote. Doing this often requires the use of an **appositive**, which not only gives the name of the person you are referencing but also tells the readers why they should care what that person has to say. There are lots of ways you can construct such a sentence, but here are a few examples:

So-and-So, the world renowned author, writes that ...

In his book, *Title Here*, So-and-So writes that....

"Some kind of quote" writes So-and-So, professor at Some University.

A renowned journalist, So-and-So claims that.....

You can, hopefully, see that the order in which you present the information doesn't matter as much as what information you are presenting. There are endless ways of creating sentences that work as citations. You just need to make sure that you are including the expert or author's name, where the quote or information is from, and what the expert's **credentials** are. You don't want to use an in-sentence citation for everything you need a citation for, and when you do use them, you want to make sure they don't get repetitive. (That means, change up the style of the sentence!) Here are a couple of other rules:

If it is the first time in the entire essay that you are referencing this source, make sure to use the author's first **and** last name. After the first time, use **only** the author's last name when you reference the source! (An exception being when you have two authors with the same last name.)

The title of a book acts as a declaration of someone's credentials: The person is an expert because of writing the book. That means you don't need to use both an appositive and the title of a book or article in an in-sentence citation.

Some instructors will still want to know the page number on which you found the quote or fact. In this case, if you use an in-sentence citation, you will still need to provide a parenthetical citation with the page number at the end of the sentence.

Do not use the words "says" or "said" when citing something that was written! You can use words like *writes, cites, claims, describes, argues, points out, asserts, states,* or any other synonym! Only use "says" or "said" if you are referencing an interview, speech, video, lecture, or some other source in which the person actually speaks.

PRACTICE EXERCISE #1

Using an appositive, convert these citations into in-sentence citations as if this were the first time you are referencing this source.

1. Stephen King, *On Writing*, "If you don't have time to read, you don't have time or the tools to write."

   _____

   _____

2. Aristotle, Greek philosopher, "The roots of education are bitter, but the fruit is sweet." _____

   _____

   _____

3. Thomas Edison, "I have not failed. I have just found 10,000 ways that didn't work." _____

   _____

   _____

4. Michael Crichton, in the forward for *Prey*, "We never seem to acknowledge that we have been wrong in the past, and so might be wrong in the future."

   _____

   _____

The second way of doing an in-text citation is much simpler. The parenthetical citation goes at the end of a sentence, just before the period. In the parenthesis should be the author's *last* name and the page number on which you found the quote or the information you are citing.

(Author #)

Please notice that there is no comma or any other punctuation in this citation. The author's first name, the title of the book or article, and an abbreviation for the word "page" (pg.) does not need to be in this citation. In that rare case that all of the information in a single paragraph comes from the same source (all of your facts, quotes, etc.) then you can place the parenthetical citation at the end of the paragraph.

PRACTICE EXERCISE #2

Identify the mistakes in the following parenthetical citations by rewriting them correctly.

1. (Tom Foolery, 5) _____

2. (Foolery, pg 7) _____

3. Foolery, Tom 8 _____

4. (Foolery, *All This*, pg 9) _____

5. (10 Foolery) _____

Quoting Tool #1: Integrating Quotes

So, you know that quotes make really great pieces of evidence and are strong support for your points. (Plus, you're required to use them!) Just what exactly are you supposed to do with them, though? Can you just plop a quote in the middle of a paragraph? Do you always have to lead in or out of a quote? How long should a quote be, anyway? These questions all have answers that depend on the circumstances. The best way to learn how to fit a quote into your essay is to pay attention to how other writers do it in the materials you are required to read. Check out the following guidelines for more direction:

> A quote must always be a complete sentence! If the quote you want to use is not a complete sentence, then you must make it a complete sentence by integrating it into a sentence of your own.

> You can use ellipses (….) to quote parts of sentences. If you are using the beginning or ending of a sentence, fill in the section you are *not* using with an ellipsis (…). If you are starting at the beginning, skipping some of the middle, and using the end, then fill in the section you are not using (the middle) with an ellipsis and period (… .).

> Sometimes a quote can stand on its own without too much explanation—if it is a complete sentence that builds on the preceding or following sentence, for example. Other times, you may need to introduce the quote (say, with an appositive or in-sentence citation), or explain it a little afterwards.

> If you need to explain a quote, do not start your next sentence with "This quote means…" or anything similar! The reader should be able to understand what the quote itself means; you just need to explain how it relates to your point!

The length of a quote will depend on how long your essay is, and what your instructor has asked you for. Keep in mind that quotes are supposed to support your own words, not replace them. So, a good "rule of thumb" is for all quoted material, combined, to be around 5% of your total word count. Of course, that could fluctuate depending on the needs of the assignment.

If you are using a quote that is longer than four lines (not just four sentences, but taking up more than four lines of your page), you will need to use a hanging indent! Ask your instructor for more info!

GRAMMAR WORKSHEET #6

Name:_____

Grammar Lesson 6: Personal Error

So far, we've looked at five common grammar problems, but surely you've been finding marks from your instructor about other sorts of problems on your graded work. Look back at the essays that have been returned to you and identify the grammar problem you've had the most trouble with. Explain why or how it is a problem, then provide an example of the mistake from your own work and show how it should be corrected.

Problem: _____

_____

_____

Explanation: _____

_____

_____

_____

_____

Example: _____

_____

_____

_____

_____

Correction: _____

_____

_____

_____

_____

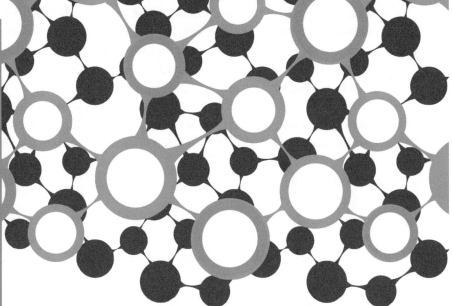

LESSON EIGHT

Research

Up until this point, we have been focusing almost solely on the process of writing: everything from sentence writing to organizing your thoughts. These are all basic skills that you need to have a good handle on in order to write an essay that achieves its goal and other people can easily understand. (In other words, a "good" essay!) However, there is more to composing that essay than doing the actual writing part. For the rest of your academic career (and maybe even further!) you will have to engage with information by first collecting it. We call the process of collecting information Research.

Research Tool #1: CRAAP

You are doubtless familiar with how to search the internet. You can search from your phone, your laptop, your PC, or whatever other device you might use to access the Web. You may use Google, Yahoo, Bing, or something else to look for information. In fact, you may have even done this to find information to use for this very class! (Ok, let's be real: you totally did!) The problem with doing a general search via one of these services, though, is that they come back with huge numbers of hits that may, or may not, actually work for what you need. On top of that, it's hard to know if any of that information is true and accurate; it could be old, or propaganda, or straight up just lies. The internet should be labeled with a warning: Buyer Beware!

So, how do you decide which websites or articles from the internet are good to use for an academic essay? You use the CRAAP Test! (As in, if it doesn't pass the test, it's crap…one of my favorite lessons!)

Current? _____

_____

_____

Relevant?_____

_____

_____

Authority? _____

_____

_____

Accurate? _____

_____

_____

Purpose? _____

_____

_____

PRACTICE EXERCISE #1

You will need to practice answering these questions for various potential sources. Eventually, you should be able to do this quickly in your head without having to process through each factor, but for now let's try this on paper. Do a quick search online for your Scrapbook topic. Put the first five results through the CRAAP Test.

1. Source _____

C _____

R _____

A _____

A _____

P _____

2. Source _____

C _____

R _____

A _____

A _____

P _____

3. Source _____

C _____

R _____

A _____

A _____

P _____

4. Source _____

C _____

R _____

A _____

A _____

P _____

5. Source _____

C _____

R _____

A _____

A _____

P _____

Research Tool #2: Academic Databases

Now, if the internet isn't the best place to get information, where are you expected to collect information from? Do you really have to read a whole book for a five- to ten-page essay? Do magazines count? What about newspapers, or YouTube videos? How about information your instructor told you in class? The truth is, those could all be valid **sources** of information, if they pass the CRAAP Test. It could take a lot of time, and effort, though, to collect all that information from such varied sources. Luckily for you, there's this thing called a library…

No matter what university, college, or other institution of education you're studying at, they are going to have some sort of library services. Even if you're taking online courses, the institution should provide you with a way to find the kind of information you're going to need in order to complete your assignments and to read about your field. At most universities and colleges, that service is provided through the library, where you can find all the books, magazines, newspapers, and other types of sources you could need.

Now, most educational libraries also have a great service meant to help you navigate the vastness of academic and professional publications, generally called databases. Why search for information in academic and professional publications? They almost invariably meet all of the CRAAP criteria. In fact, those sources are so reliable, you can pretty much skip the whole CRAAP Test step in the research process. Almost all of these professional publications put forth a lot of effort to make sure that what they're publishing is true, accurate, unbiased, and current. Perfect, right?

NOTE . . . .

So, how do you get to this treasure hold of information? You will have to access your university's library page, then find the link for databases. If you're having trouble, ask your instructor, go the library's physical location and ask for help, access online tutorials, or use Web chat, instant messaging, or even texting services!

There are many different databases. Some of them are subject specific, like Biology or Literature. Some of them cast a wider net, searching whatever your university has access to for your search terms. Some of them come with complex search pages, where you can limit your search parameters to something very specific, and others have more generic search pages with only a few options. All of them will search through articles published in the academic journals, newspapers, or magazines that your university has paid subscriptions for. (Part of your tuition at work!) Since each database is unique, there is no one-fits-all lesson that will allow you to use any database you choose perfectly. However, we can look at a basic example of one of the most popular databases, Academic Search Complete, which uses an Ebsco search page.

Please navigate to that page now. If you are not in a computer lab classroom or do not have access to a computer with internet capabilities, please refer to your instructor's directions. If you have not been given instruction on how to navigate to your institution's library database system, please ask your instructor for further information.

List some of the options for specifying your search:

1. _____ 2. _____

3. _____ 4. _____

5. _____ 6. _____

Which of these options do you believe is most important to set and why? _____

_____

_____

_____

_____

_____

_____

When you are running a search, the options you should always set are limiting by date, type of publication, type of document, language, length, and "full text." How you set them will depend on what you are looking for and what your instructor has told you to do. Here are my standard recommendations:

1. Limit for a recent date. Generally speaking, "recent" in the academic world means the past ten years.

2. Choose a type of document, like a periodical (a journal or magazine).

3. Choose "article" under document

© fatmawati achmad zaenuri /Shutterstock.com

type. Abstracts and bibliographies are rarely useful.

4. Pick how many pages you are actually willing to read. Don't lie to yourself, if it's only three, limit for three!

5. Always click the option for pdf full text! This ensures that you can actually *read* whatever hits you get! You will also get the benefit of seeing whatever graphs or images may have originally appeared with the article, rather than only seeing the words written.

After you've limited your parameters, conducting your search should feel pretty familiar. Usually, you can apply several terms. Notice at the top of the Ebsco search page that there are options for how your search terms are linked. For example, you can choose "and," asking the engine to look for both words in your search, or "not," asking the engine to look for one word, but not the other. You can also tell the engine where to look for your search terms by choosing a field. (Usually, the options are In the Text or Title, for example.) Here are a couple more tricks:

© fatmawati achmad zaenuri /Shutterstock.com

> If you want two or more words to appear exactly as you type them, put quotation marks around the words. For example, you might search for "gender bias" or "school lunch." Instead of searching for each term separately, the engine will only look for sources where those two (or more) words appear in exactly that order.

> If you want to include all variations of a word, you can type in the root of the word and then apply an asterisk. For example, you could look for child*, which will then also search for words like "children" or "childhood." You can also click the "Apply Related Words" option, which will ask the engine to search for synonyms for the terms you provide.

Access Academic Search Complete (or whichever database your instructor prefers) via your institution's website. Limit using the parameters just listed. For search terms, use _____ and _____. Answer the following questions.

1. What is the title of the article in the third result? _____

_____

2. Who is the author (or first author) of the first result? _____

_____

3. Is there an abstract provided for the fourth result? _____

_____

4. Where was the second result published? _____

_____

NOTE ·

Most databases can do other helpful things, like save your searches, email you search results or specific articles, even generate copy/paste-ready citations! For more info or help, ask your instructor or contact a librarian!

ESSAY 4

Essay Mode—Expository Analysis

In most classes you take, you will be asked to gather information (reading or attending lectures, for example), make connections between those pieces of information, and respond by demonstrating a new or better understanding of a topic based on the information. At this point in the semester, you have learned many valuable tools to help you write academically, from reading tools to thinking tools. Now it is time to start putting those together.

The purpose of the expository analysis is to demonstrate a deeper understanding of your topic. You want to show your instructor that you gathered information about a particular topic, you thought about that information from as many angles as you could think of, paying particular attention to the way pieces of information fit together, and that you came away with a new understanding of the topic.

JOURNAL 4

Write the definitions for the words that label this type of essay.
Expose –
Analyze –
How does this help you understand the purpose of the essay?

For this essay, you are going to be looking at the connections in a cause and effect relationship. Some cause/effect relationships are very easy to understand.

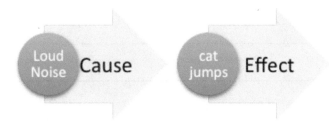

In this case, a loud noise causes the cat to jump. The loud noise is the **cause**, and the cat jumping is the **effect**. However, not all cause/effect relationships are so simple. Often there are many causes for a particular effect, and likewise there are often many effects of a particular cause. Sometimes, you can start with a particular thing, an event for example, and trace back its many causes, then trace forward its many effects.

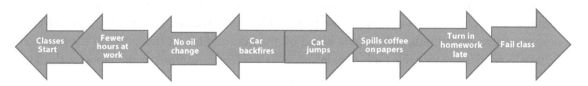

As you can see, even this is pretty straight forward. You could start asking all kinds of questions, like "Why did classes starting lead to having fewer hours at work?" or "Why did turning in one assignment late lead to failure of the course?" Those answers would probably lead you to more branches on the cause/effect relationship. That's because doing this with real life is pretty hard—life is, after all, pretty complicated. Let's practice.

PRACTICE EXERCISE #1

Directions: Choose a momentous event in your life (high school graduation, starting college, etc.). First, trace back the major events that had to occur in order for that momentous event to happen. Then, trace forward (using your imagination perhaps) all of the major events that will happen (or did happen) because of that momentous event. Use the words "because" and "caused."

Causes

_____

_____

_____

_____

_____

_____

Effects

_____

_____

_____

_____

_____

_____

PRACTICE EXERCISE #2

Hopefully you were able to see that there are many causes and effects of every moment and that they all exist in relation to each other. Let's try this with something even more difficult though. Tracing the causes and effects of states of being can be even trickier. Read the following example.

In the mid 1600s, as navigation, ship building, medicine, and food preservation became better, more and more trade developed between Europe and other parts of the world. Soon, Europeans began drinking large quantities of tea, which is caffeinated. The extra caffeine allowed many people to think more quickly and gave them more energy for extra activities after work, such as reading. Thusly, the "common" population became more educated, which allowed them to understand that their governments were abusing them. In the mid-1700s, the people of some English colonies on the eastern coast of North America declared themselves independent of Britain and established their own country.

Now, answer the following questions.

1. What one main cause led to what main effect? _____

   _____

2. What would you identify as the "middle" point, where the causes "end" and the "effects" begin?

   _____

3. What words indicated that there was a cause/effect relationship being described here? Were the words "cause" or "effect" ever used?

_____

_____

4. What "state of being" is being analyzed here? _____

_____

_____

PRACTICE EXERCISE #3: GUIDED PREP

For this essay, you will be asked to pick your own topic. Picking a topic is one of the more challenging parts of writing an essay. You must pick a topic that not only has to do with the class you are taking, but also one that is both academic and of the correct breadth for the number of pages or word count you are being asked to write. To help you out, I have given you "umbrella" subjects. You must choose a topic that falls under one of these umbrellas. In the space below each umbrella, start to brainstorm a couple of ideas for topics.

<u>Education</u>
What are some issues facing education today? How are these issues related to each other? What other issues (political, cultural, etc.) might also be related? Why do you think these issues exist? Are they issues facing other countries or cultures? What do you think should be done about them?

Discrimination

What are some issues facing our culture today? (Think broadly and creatively; don't limit yourself to gender or race.) Why are people discriminatory? Where do these problems come from? How can an individual become less discriminatory? How can a culture become less discriminatory?

Food and Eating Habits

What are some issues facing our culture today? What aspects of our culture influence our eating habits? Who do you think is responsible? How or why do you think these habits or standards developed? What other things are effected by food and eating habits?

Expository Analysis

GOALS:

Demonstrate a fully faceted comprehension of a particular issue

Demonstrate an ability to select an appropriate academic topic

Demonstrate an ability to utilize appropriate sources

Demonstrate an ability to draw connections between several sources and to extrapolate original ideas

Demonstrate a collegiate level of writing (organization, sentence structure, punctuation, etc.)

DIRECTIONS:

Analyze multiple dimensions of a particular issue. You may focus your essay around identifying problems, discussing the effects of those problems, suggesting solutions, or a combination of those things. It is important to clearly state the connections you've made mentally between the pieces of information you've read that have led you to these conclusions. Your analysis will **_not_** be based on another person's ideas, but on the connections you have made. You must use logic and evidence in such a way that the reader will be able to come to the same conclusion you have. You must use at least three academic sources to support your points. Remember that this is not an argument. You are not trying to convince the reader that you are correct. You are only presenting the information you have collected in such a way as to show the connections between facts. Your language must remain objective; do not refer to yourself, to class, or to your own essay.

TIPS:

Start with Bubbles to draw connections between articles and ideas.

Try drawing a timeline or using arrows to see the pattern of causes/effects.

Use extensive annotation while reading/keep notes during class discussions.

Create a detailed outline to plot out your organization of ideas.

REQUIREMENTS:

- _____ words
- Reference as least three academic sources
- Utilize three to four quotes of various lengths
- Include a works cited page

© Ron Leishman/Shutterstock.com

PRACTICE: STUDENT ESSAY #4

Name:_____

Here is the student example of an expository analysis essay to help you understand what you should be doing. Keep in mind that this is a real example, and so it is not "perfect." Follow the directions to help you analyze the example.

Student Essay Evaluation
Expository Analysis

Directions:

In yellow, highlight sentences that express the main points.
In pink, highlight cause/effect information.
In green, highlight any vocabulary you are unfamiliar with.
Circle with a pen any grammatical or punctuation mistakes you find.

1. What main subject is the essay analyzing? _____

_____

2. Does the author use good essay structure? Why/how? _____

_____

3. What types of evidence does the author provide?_____

_____

_____

_____

_____

_____

4. What conclusions do you think the author is trying to draw you to? Are they making an argument?

_____

_____

_____

_____

_____

Ewelina Siwik
Essay #4
Due: 11/4/15
Words 802

The rise of the GMO's

"In the U.S., GMOs are in as much as 80% of conventional processed food." (The Non-GMO Project) GMO stands for Genetically Modified Organism, which is a living organism that has had its genetic material artificially manipulated in laboratories with the help of genetic engineering. (GE) GMOs have caused controversy worldwide, which leads to the Food Safety Unit of the World Health Organization as well as the regulatory authorities in the U.S. and Europe to conduct investigations to get better insight of GMOs. Society has also recently become more aware of GMOs due to the fact that many large corporations are responsible for producing and selling GMO products. GMOs have become so mainstream that they have begun to take an increasing toll on society. GMOs are known to cause health risks and devastate rural economies, but there are positives effects such as production of more food and adjustment to climate change.

The genetic engineering component is a major health risk of GMOs that causes dangerous side effects. Combining genes of different species to produce a whole new species unleashes various erratic allergic reactions in people. Otherwise, if the species were not genetically engineered together, they probably would not cause any reaction on their own. Another health risk of GMOs is that they have the potential to produce disease-causing bacteria resistant to current antibiotics, which can overall increase the spread of infections and diseases in people. "Over 80% of all GMOs grown worldwide are engineered for herbicide tolerance." (The Non-GMO Project) Essentially, GMO food contains "antibiotic resistance makers" which help the producers recognize if the genetically modified material actually conveyed into the host food. The FDA (Food Drug Administration) was a key member in introducing the antibiotic marker into the food supply. If this antibiotic marker impacts the majority of the food it will extinguish the necessary antibiotics to fight serious diseases. For example, a GMO corn plant contains an ampicillin-resistance gene. Ampicillin is a very beneficial antibiotic used to handle an assortment of infections in people and animals. (U.S. National Library of Medicine) As the ampicillin resistance gene progresses from the corn plant to humans, this causes ampicillin to become less effective at battling a variety of bacterial infections. The financial burden linked with farmers planting GMO crops is quite steep. The significant difference is the amount it takes to purchase the seed; it costs about one hundred fifty dollars more to purchase a GMO seed than just any regular seed (modernfarmer.com). Other financial burdens that come along with GMO crops are the increase of spending more on chemicals due to the fear of a new weed. With the market moving more towards non-GMO foods, most biotech companies and food companies are forced to label GMOs, which then turns consumers against many products from that many companies and farmers lose profit as well as income.

GMOs do just as much good as they do bad, though they help fight malnutrition and climate change. As population increases, so does the abundant third world hunger; poor nutrition causes about nearly 45% of deaths in children under five which accumulates to 3.1 million children each year (Food and Agriculture Organization of the United Nations). The use of GMOs can help increase major food groups required to help humans survive, such as golden rice. A new strain of GMO golden rice comes from a series of viruses and daffodils, which produce beta carotene that the human body typically transforms to vitamin A. Consuming rice such as this can help defend against blindness and death especially in starving children. (Huffington Post) GMO plants also help produce crops that are improved to withstand climate change, including threats of drought, disease, and insect infestation. Farmers have the ability to grow crops in a larger scale of areas all over the world. GMOs have also helped decrease soil erosion by ninety percent, which overall preserves thirty-seven million tons of topsoil. (USDA) For example, a new variety of potato can be produced a lot more efficiently if necessary to adapt to a sudden change in climate temperature. Generally, it takes about fifteen years to produce a new organic sort of potato, but compared to a GMO modified potato only takes six months. GMO plant breeders have the capability to adjust more exact changes and pull from a larger source of genes and from plants organisms.

Overall, there are many outlets of information to promote or discontinue the use of genetically modified organisms. GMOs have a multitude of effects which can be considered a positive input on society or negative. Positive usage of GMOs includes the ability to conquer and end world hunger also relive farmers of climate change issues. Then again, the negative usage of GMOs can increase serious health risks as well as devastate rural economies.

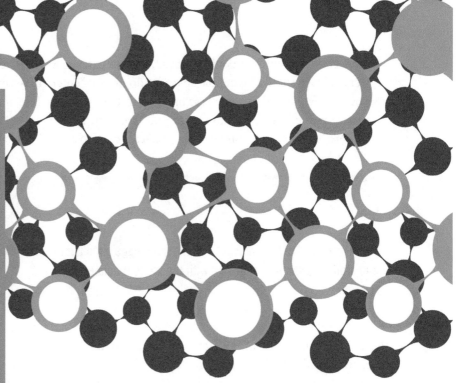

LESSON NINE

Works Cited Pages

To set up a works cited page, here are some basic rules:

1. The works cited page is always the last page of your document. It is always on its own page.
2. The works cited page should be numbered accordingly with the rest of your document.
3. The margins of the works cited page should be the same as the rest of your document.
4. The font should also be the same as the rest of your document.
5. The words "Works Cited" should be at the very top, centered. They should not be underlined, italicized, or in a different font or different size from any of the rest of the text.
6. All of your entries should appear in alphabetical order, according to author's last name. If more than one author is listed, use the first author listed. If there is no author, use the first word of the title.

7. All entries should be double spaced, but no extra spacing is required between entries. (The entire page should be double spaced—do not hit "enter" between entries.)
8. All entries should use a reverse hanging indent—the first line of each entry should begin at the margin line, and each subsequent line should be indented one "tab."
9. There is no need to number your entries. You also should not use bullet points.

NOTE ·

If you need an example of what a works cited page should look like, please go back through the book and study the samples provided with the student essays!

These basic rules help you format your works cited page, but they don't tell you anything about what the citations themselves should look like. The rules for these citations are pretty specific, and they vary depending on what citation style you are using (MLA, APA, CMS, etc.). Luckily for you, most database services provide an automatic citation generation option so that all you have to do is copy/paste the citation into your document. Many other services frequently used for academic purposes, such as Google Scholar and BrainyQuote, will do the same. If you find yourself having to generate a citation from scratch, you may turn to an online service such as KnightCite.com, CitationMachine, or EasyBib. If you use one of these services, make sure you:

© Aha-Soft/Shutterstock.com

1. Use the proper citation style (MLA, APA, CMS, etc.)
2. Choose the right type of citation (article, book, etc.)
3. Reformat the indenting once you've copied it into your own document

There are only about five types of citations you will probably need to cite at this point in your academic career. There are citation guidelines for just about anything you could want to use in an academic article, from songs to videos to images, however, these are the five most common:

Book. This refers to an entire book. If you have read and referenced an entire book, you will want to cite the entire thing. However, there is also an option for citing only part of a book, usually labeled as a "selection from a book" or "a chapter from a book."

Article from an academic journal or periodical. This refers to the type of sources you will most often find on those databases we talked about. You will need to have specific information about the page numbers on which the article is found and the volume or issue number of the journal it was found in. There are also special options for when you have used a database to find those articles, so you will need to specify that you found the article "electronically" or via "database" and be prepared with the date you found it and the name of the database you used.

Anthology. This refers to a book that contains numerous articles or stories by various authors. Most often you will need to cite a "Selection from an Anthology." These books are especially popular in literature, English, composition, and history courses.

Website. This refers to an entire website. If you have used only one page or one article from a website, there are specific guidelines for how you cite that as well.

Article from a newspaper or magazine. This is fairly self-explanatory, but you will have to specify whether you found the article online or in print. Also, this does not refer to a professional or academic journal, but more mainstream publications such as *Time, Popular Mechanics,* or *People.*

NOTE ·

For a complete reference to all the types of citations you might need to use and what information you will need to generate them, check out OWLPurdue at https://owl.english.purdue.edu. It is an amazing source for any composition questions you might have about MLA or APA style, avoiding plagiarism, and even grammar! Use the handy search bar to find exactly what you need without sifting through a bunch of information you don't!

PRACTICE EXERCISE #1

Convert the following information into proper citations for a works cited page. Use whatever handbook or source your instructor prefers. (Note: None of these items, with the exception of *Supersize Me*, are real. These are all fictitious sources made up for the sole purpose of practicing this skill.)

Title: The Happy Memories Club
Author: Lee Smith
Anthology: Modern Asian-American Voices
Pg. Numbers: 481-492
Editor: Michael Meyer
Publisher: Bedford/St. Martins
Year: 2009
City: Boston

_____

_____

_____

Title: The Other in Shakespeare: A Study of Othello, The Merchant of Venice, and The Tempest
Author: Seth Innis
Journal: Shakespeare Quarterly
Pg. Numbers: 42-56
Volume: 6
Issue: 2
Year: 2008

_____

_____

_____

Title: GhostShells
Author: J.L. Scott
Publisher: Penguin
Year: 2010
City: New York

_____

_____

_____

Title: Stephen Hawking: Physicist and Dreamer
Author: Dr. Stephen Hawking
Editor: Brad Butler
Sponsor: MIT
Date Published: 1997
URL: http://www.hawking.org.uk
Date Accessed: today

_____

_____

_____

Title: Self-Consciousness
Author: Dr. Benjamin Wallace
Anthology: Consciousness: A Psychological Overview
Pg. Numbers: 856-920
Editor: Albert Bandura and Phyllis Hammer
Publisher: Harrington Inc.
Year: 2002
City: Chicago

_____

_____

_____

Title: Supersize Me
Writer: Morgan Spurlock
Director: Morgan Spurlock
Produced: Kathbur Pictures
Date: May 21, 2004

_____

_____

_____

© matrioshika/Shuttestock.com

Essay Mode—Argument

I'm sure you know what the term "argument" means. You can argue with your parents, your siblings, your friends, even strangers. You believe one thing, they believe something else. Emotions get involved, maybe you even start yelling at each other.

This isn't that.

An argumentative essay is not an opinion. Yes, you should believe what you are arguing, therefore making it your opinion, but where an opinion can be held without factual evidence, an argumentative essay can not. An argumentative essay must also be…well, an essay. Which means that it must be academic, organized, and unbiased. This makes it different from a persuasive essay as well. In a persuasion, the only goal is to convince your audience to agree with you, and there are all kinds of techniques you can utilize to do that. While the ultimate goal of an argumentative essay is the same, to convince your reader of your point, the techniques used are limited to relaying factual information (evidence) and outlining the logic you've used to come to your conclusions.

Generally speaking, students tell me this is the easiest of the essays to write because it seems to be easier to tell people what they should think or do. We all like to be right! And we all like to tell other people what to do. The trick is to do it without being condescending or aggressive. That starts with picking a topic that can be argued academically and without bias. You may believe, for example, that aliens exist. That's fine, but since you can't prove it, it doesn't work well as an academic argument (at least, not for this type of class—perhaps for a philosophy class or maybe a statistics class). Therefore, your topic must be relevant to the course.

Let's work on this.

PRACTICE EXERCISE #1

Of the assertions listed, decide if each would work as either an academic essay or an opinion.
1. No woman should ever serve as president of the United States.
2. Everybody should be required to carry health insurance.
3. The practice of prostitution by adults should be legalized.
4. Drug users and people convicted of violent crimes should not have children.
5. College athletes should not have to attend classes.
6. Homework should not be assigned to children in elementary school.

You noticed, hopefully, that all of the assertions listed had something in common; they all used the word "should." You should remember from our work on thesis statements, that an assertion always has a strong word at its core. In an argument, the most common word used is "should" (or "should not") because strong arguments often call for change. The assertion could be calling for a change in policy, belief, law, practice, or even habit. You do not *have* to use the word "should." Sometimes the word "is" or its negative works very well, too. However, you should check whether your assertion is making an argument for change or not before you begin doing your prep work.

PRACTICE EXERCISE #2: GUIDED PREP

You have studied a number of topics this semester, both in this class and in others. Additionally, I'm sure there were many cultural and political events that occurred which may have caught your attention. On the lines here, write out some of the topics you found most interesting.

_____   _____

_____   _____

_____   _____

_____   _____

Now, narrow that list down to three options. On the lines here, write out possible argumentative assertions that could be linked to those options.

_____

_____

_____

_____

_____

_____

Will any of those assertions work for this essay assignment? Use the space below to do some brainstorming. Try using a concept map to work out what your main supports would be.

Argument

GOALS:

Demonstrate an ability to use vocabulary and language appropriately
Demonstrate an ability to create flow and unity through structure and organization
Demonstrate an ability to draw together information from multiple sources for one essay
Demonstrate a collegiate level of writing (sentence structure, punctuation, etc.)

DIRECTIONS:

Write an argumentative essay on a topic of interest to you. Essentially, convince me of something. Topics must be approved by the instructor. Your assertion should be something that any reasonable person could argue with. Use logic and evidence to support your claim in such a way that your reader may come to believe your assertion. You must use at least five academic articles. You may use up to two additional sources as needed. Remember to remain objective (no personal pronouns). An argument is NOT a personal opinion, but a stance on an issue that can be supported with outside evidence.

TIPS:

Start with your assertion.
Make a list of reasons "why."

REQUIREMENTS:

- _____ words
- Reference as least five academic articles and as many as seven sources in total
- Utilize four to six quotes of various lengths as support or demonstration of main points
- Include a works cited page

© Rudi Strummer/Shutterstock.com

PRACTICE: STUDENT ESSAY #5

Name_____

Here is a student example of an argumentative essay to help you understand what you should be doing. Keep in mind that this is a real example, and so it is not "perfect." Follow the directions to help you analyze the example.

Directions:
> In yellow, highlight the thesis statement.
> In pink, highlight each topic sentence or main point.
> In blue, highlight the argument words used.
> In green, highlight any vocabulary you are unfamiliar with.
> Circle with a pen any grammatical or punctuation mistakes you find.

Answer the following:

1. What is the assertion? _____

_____

2. Can you identify the structure for this essay? _____

_____

3. List the writer's main supporting points.

_____

_____

4. Has the writer's argument convinced you? Why or why not?_____

_____

Erika Frazee

Essay #4

October 30, 2015

804 Word Count

Overweight and On The Go

In a fast paced world, people are speeding through life so fast all they have time to do is grow; not in a good way either. Americans are growing in numbers very rapidly in count, and on the scale. "68.8 percent of American adults age 20 and older are overweight or obese" (NIH). With Americans living such busy fast pace lives, they do not have time to eat properly or exercise enough.

In America, people are not slowing down to make time to eat. They are not cooking meals properly. Americans are resorting to box meals that contain preservatives and high amounts of sodium and cholesterol. "In the 1.2 trillion dollar food market, Americans are spending 5 billion dollars on low cost boxed food products" (Segran). This number is growing every year. Most of the preserved box meals have little to no nutritional value for the consumer. This type of behavior is closely related to Americans belief that time is money. People do not want to spend between one to three hours in the kitchen for two meals a day. Americans do not have the time. "The average box meal takes about five to twelve minutes to cook, where as cooking a full healthy meal with variety and portion control takes about forty-five minutes to two hours" (Segran). Which in todays age, Americans try to preserve any time possible, even risking health issues. This pressure to save time and live a fast paced life is causing Americans to become overweight.

Americans are also consuming high amounts of fast food in order to save time. Along with eating a lot of boxed meals Americans diets also consist of fast food restaurant chains. Americans love the concepts of drive through fast food pick up windows. Americans like the idea of being able to stay in their cars to get food and eat it on the go in their car. "McDonald›s feeds about 45 million people around the world every day" (Kidd). McDonald's only accounts for a tiny portion of the fast food consumed around the world. Americans alone spend 1 billion dollars of fast food a year. This large amount of people consuming fast food is leading to obesity. One meal at a fast food restaurant contains all the calories you need for an entire day." If you eat a Big Mac, large fries, and large Coke, you will have to walk non-stop for six hours to burn off the calories you have gained" (Kidd). It is better to eat more small meals a day then to eat one or two large meals a day. That way the body can digest its food and burn more fat. Americans are always on the go. This means, they do not have time to eat many small meals a day. "The average American eats two meals a day and retains about 2,600 calories" (Segan). Which to obtain a healthy life and consume the proper amount of calories, someone who is 5'7, 150 pounds should take in 1,500 calories and burn 250-300 off a day doing moderate exercise (NIH). If Americans would slow down their paced of life and make time to eat healthy meals and exercise then this problem would slowly start to decrease.

Americans are not making time for exercise. Along with eating high sodium and sugar filled diets people are also avoiding exercise. "The average person is suggested to get 30 minutes of moderate to high intensity work outs a day, but studies show that only 38 percent of Americans are exercising at the rate they should be" (Laskowski). This is an alarming number when 68 percent of America is overweight or obese. Americans have a modern way of life, save as much time as possible and try to cram as much into their day as possible. Then, when they get home the average American watches five hours of television a day. Scheduling and squeezing every minute out of every day just to go home and eat a boxed dinner and watch reruns of an old television series is not the best use for Americans time. "Just by cutting down

the time Americans watch T.V by 2 hours and using that amount of time to exercise and eat a healthy meal each day, Americans could cut down the obesity rate by about three percent in one year" (Laskowski).

If Americans do not make time to eat healthy and cook proper meals the grim reality is that most people will be suffering real health concerns. Americans need to take the time to exercise and eat healthy meals in healthy portions. Stop letting the fast food industries take over their fast pace life. If Americans change their busy schedules, they may have a longer life instead.

Works Cited

Hinkley, David. "Average American Watches 5 Hours of TV per Day." *NY Daily News*. David Hinkley, Mar. 2015. Web. 30 Oct. 2015.

Lowcowski, Edward R., M.D. "Fitness." *Exercise: How Much Do I Need Every Day?* N.p., 2015. Web. 30 Oct. 2015.

"Overweight and Obesity Statistics." *Overweight and Obesity Statistics*. NIH, 1 May 2012. Web. 30 Oct. 2015.

"Shocking Fast Food Statistics You Should Know." *Shocking Fast Food Statistics You Should Know*. Ohio Medical Group, Feb. 2015. Web. 30 Oct. 2015.

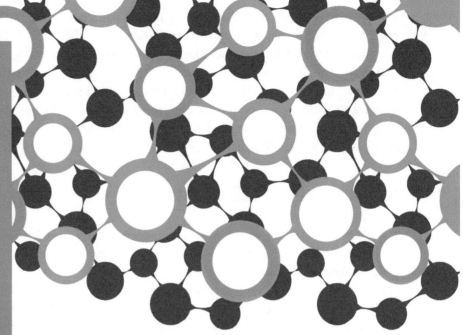

Elements of the
Essay: Conclusion

Have you ever heard a song on the radio, maybe one you only have heard once or twice before, and even though you aren't too familiar with it you know that the end is coming within a few seconds? That's a fairly common experience because we all have schema, or mental parameters, for things like songs and music which tell us that the end of a song will sound a certain way. Now, that could be all kinds of different things, but in general if you ask several people from the same culture what the end of a song sounds like, they're likely to come up with a pretty cohesive list of characteristics.

The end of your essay should have a similar feeling. A reader should be able to get a sense that you have made all of your points and are going to finish your essay, even without skipping ahead to see that the pages end and you obviously haven't written any more. We use the last section of your essay to do that, which is called the **conclusion**. It is called the conclusion because that is where you (duh duh duh!) draw a conclusion! In this section of your essay, you should not only reference each of your main points and thesis, but you should also make some kind of statement that draws everything together. Now, you may think that you shouldn't have to do that. After all, didn't you just spend your whole essay connecting everything together? Sure, but remember your repetition pattern: Tell me what you're going to tell me, tell me, then tell me what you just told me. The conclusion is the last part of your GPS that usually reads something like: "You have arrived at your destination!"

Conclusion Tool #1: Elements

Just like your introduction, and your essay as whole, there are three elements to a conclusion. Unlike in an introduction or your essay as a whole, however, these elements do not need to appear in a specific order. You can get creative with your conclusion, including whatever information you want to remain foremost in your readers' minds. However, since people are most likely to remember best whatever they read last, make sure you include:

1. Your assertion from your thesis
2. Reference to your main points
3. An answer to the question, "Why was this important?"

Although you could simply copy/paste your assertion into your conclusion, and follow that up with simple sentences restating your main points, you need to be very careful not to seem repetitive. Mixing in other elements, like an unused shocking statistic or startling quote, can help cement your conclusion in the readers' minds.

The last element is probably the most important. Although it may seem like the importance of your topic is pretty obvious to you, some readers might need help making that connection. Certain topics *will* have an obvious importance: topics that are culturally or politically popular at the time, or topics about human rights, for instance. In those cases, you may need to state why it should be important specifically to your readers, so make it personal. If the topic is important to you, but may not necessarily be important to anyone else, then this is where you get the chance to explain why it is important and other people should care about it just as much as you!

PRACTICE EXERCISE #1

Use the following thesis statement to write a conclusion paragraph. You can make up statistics or quotes to support yourself. Answer the critical thinking questions first to help you out!

As gender inequality is increasingly highlighted as a civil rights issue in the United States, politicians need to be more open to drafting policies targeting transgender rights, female reproductive health rights, and male parental rights.

1. What mode of essay is this? _____

   _____

2. What stand do you think the author is making? _____

   _____

   _____

3. What are the author's main points? _____

   _____

4. What information, or RENNS, do you think the author might have included in the essay?

   _____

   _____

   _____

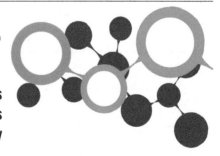

JOURNAL 5

Reflect on the semester. Write about the most important things you have learned. You can write about things you learned in this class, in other classes, or not in a class at all. Think carefully about what skills you have learned, more so than information.

Essay Mode—Synthesis

In the context of essay writing, a synthesis is a mode in which you combine many elements. While in this course and perhaps other composition courses you have been asked to write in specific modes, it is uncommon in other courses to be asked to write such narrowly defined essays. In fact, much of the time you'll be asked to simply "write a seven-page essay" with very little direction on what your topic should be or in what mode or style you should write. Sometimes, people have more difficulty with less direction than they do when they are given very specific directions.

To help you overcome some of the difficulty of an ambiguous assignment, you should ask what your instructor's expectations are for the work. Not only does that make you a good student, but in the end it will help you get a better grade!

PRACTICE EXERCISE #1

In the space here, write out some questions you think would be good to ask your instructor when you are given an ill-defined assignment. (Leave room to jot down ideas from classmates and your current instructor!)

1. _____

   _____

2. _____

   _____

3. _____

   _____

4. _____

   _____

5. _____

_____

6. _____

_____

7. _____

_____

8. _____

_____

9. _____

_____

10. _____

_____

Once you have a clear understanding of what the assignment is, you can start to do your prep work. Don't forget that reading and annotating are the first step to prep. You should be doing that throughout the semester, just as you have been doing your scrapbook assignments. For this last essay, you will be using your scrapbook topic and articles. You will be asked to combine the different types of modes into a single essay. In order to do that, you will need to pick out some important information.

GUIDED PREP

Answer these questions to help you prepare for your last essay.

1. Why was this topic interesting/important to you when you first started reading about it?

   _____

   _____

   _____

   _____

2. How has your perception or understanding of this topic changed as you have read?

   _____

   _____

   _____

   _____

3. Besides being about the same topic, in what ways are the articles you read related?

   _____

   _____

   _____

   _____

Scrapbook Synthesis

GOALS:

To effectively integrate different writing styles into a single essay

DIRECTIONS:

This semester, you have written five different types of essays. A really good essay, however, will often incorporate pieces of each style. For this assignment, write an overview (summary with some notes of critique and comment on credibility of sources), an analysis (cause/effect, compare/contrast, etc.) and a section in which you discuss what you now think about the topic and provide some sort of argument. Use between five and seven of your scrapbook articles for your sources.

THE GOOD NEWS:

This is a less formal assignment. Therefore, you <u>may</u> use first person (me, my, I). For this assignment, we are taking our first steps toward developing voice, so it is important to develop a personal sense of writing style; however, be careful to only use it appropriately. You must still remain as objective as possible and should remain unbiased.

© Scott Richardson/Shutterstock.com

REQUIREMENTS:

- _____ words
- Four to five appropriate quotes
- Works cited page (only for sources actually cited within your text)

PRACTICE – STUDENT ESSAY #6

Name:_____

Here is the student example of a synthesis essay to help you understand what you should be doing. Keep in mind that this is a real example, and so it is not "perfect." Follow the directions to help you analyze the example.

DIRECTIONS:

In yellow, highlight the thesis statement.
In pink, highlight the beginning of each new section indicating a mode.
In green, highlight any vocabulary you are unfamiliar with.
Circle with a pen any grammatical or punctuation mistakes you find.

Answer the following:

1. Identify the student's scrapbook topic. _____

_____

2. What percentage of the essay does each mode take up?

___ Summary/Critique   ___ Analysis

___ Definition   ___ Argument

3. What transitions did the student use to tie each section together as a whole?

_____

_____

4. What was the purpose of combining the different types of essays? What effect did it have?

_____

_____

Vince Lester

Essay 5

4/15/2015

Word Count: 1,368

Radio Impacting Society

The invention of the radio has changed society. Many people do not realize how often they use the radio. While it was more popular in the past, it is still making a comeback. While internet radio stations like Pandora or Spotify are booming, traditional is more popular than people think. One can listen to it on their drive to work or listening to at the gym or even at work. Traditional radio such as music dj shifts or even talk radio has changed society. Back in the day, radio was the source of entertainment such as comedy shows, and any new music. Radio was the first kind of media to have commercials and have an entertainment type shows. Radio coined the term "soap operas" as well. Radio has impacted the lives of everyday people and has changed society.

The articles that were reviewed were very insightful. They contained information on the history of how radio came about as well as how it is used today. Some articles contained information on how it was used in the past years as well. It was eye opening and it was clear that in the past years radio was one of the most popular sources of news and entertainment, as well as its other uses. In the article titled "Becoming Modern: America In the 20's" from the website "America In Class" states "Radio features shows such as bed time stories." It was a different article that was interesting. Most of the articles summed up how radio was invented and how it came to the radio we know today. The best articles were "How Radio Changed Everything" by Guy Gugliotta and "Understanding Media & Culture" by Jack Lule. These articles clearly laid out how radio has changed our culture. The articles had very interesting facts on how radio began and simple ways people use radio today. They were written very professionally and they were easy to follow. All of the articles had their strong points and their weak points. The weakness of the articles would have to be the organization that was used. First they would talk about the history then they would talk about the first radio station and then go back to the history. Other than that most of the articles that were reviewed had insightful information on the topic.

When the wireless telegraphy also known as the radio was invented by Guglielmo Marconi in the 19th century, it has only impacted our culture since. Author of "How Radio Changed Or Lives" Hamad Almuhanna states, "Radio Has been one of the most popular methods of communication." Radio was the type of media that many people received their information, from sports to presidential announcements to local happenings. In the 19th century the radio became affordable to almost everyone. Almuhanna also states "Radio could be easily bought and therefore had become common in almost every household in America." With that being said the content being broadcasted received a lot of ratings because that was what everyone was doing, listening to the radio. Families would sit together in the family room and listen to a radio program. Not only were there entertainment shows to listen to, but there were also educational shows that one could listen to. Deanna Stefanyshyn, author of "The Influence of Radio and Television" states, Radio allowed information to be distributed to a much larger audience. Radio as an educational tool become popular and many studies proved its effectiveness, especially in the area of distance education." The types of education shows would involve "How to" type shows or classroom type shows. Radio was heavily used by our Government as well. Once the Government heard about the radio they had to use it. Guy Gugliotta, author of "How Radio Changed Everything" states, "Governments started to understands radio's immense potential, not only for communications but also as a weapon: radio detecting and ranging, better known as radar." The U.S used the radio or radar mostly in the Second World War. Not only has radio impacted everyday citizens but it has impacted our Government and has helped us communicate and win a World War. The music aspect of radio made the medium popular. It helped the careers of musicians soar. People today use radio as a way to pass time at work or in the car. When the invention of the television came, it used some of the aspects of that radio had such as commercials and entertainment shows. Radio has also impacted society by keeping individuals informed on certain events. Events such as what is happening in your town or city. Also radio was used to broadcast presidential results. So in that sense politics used radio quite a bit. Talk radio shows have grown in the past years. People like Howard Stern or Rush Limbaugh have made a profitable living on their talk radio show. People have used radio for entertainment purposes, government issues, politics, and educational purposes.

The invention of the radio should be recognized as a popular media outlet as well as its impact on society. Many people today do not realize how popular radio was in the past decades. It was so popular that whatever was broadcasted, people instantly thought it was the truth. For example, in the 1930's Orson Wells broadcasted a dramatic reading of0 *War of the Worlds*. It was a story about aliens invading and many people who listened to the broadcast believed it to be the truth. That goes to show that it was very popular at the time. Today that type of shows is not as popular because the music shows gain the most followings. Guy Gugliotta also states in his article "How Radio Changed Everything," "Engineers keep finding more and more uses for radio, and frequencies never seem to und up on the scrap heap." So not only do people use it for their drive to work or for their work out but engineers use it for their work. Stations around the country use radio to broadcast their views and ideas, whether if it is a morning talk show or even a music show. In the music show the DJ could give his or her views during their talking segment. Radio has become a great way to communicate to people because it is still used today. Internet radio stations that are booming still need to make money, so they still have commercials. It does not seem like internet radio has as much commercials, but they do have them. People who are on the radio today seemed to like the medium because only their voice is being broadcasted not their looks. Jack Lule, author of "Understanding Media & Culture" states that "Radio encouraged the growth of national popular music stars and brought regional sounds to wider audiences. The effects of early radio programs can be felt both in modern popular music and in television programming." Radio has the power to make songs famous, and make songs annoying. Radio had comedy shows, dramatic soap operas, as well as scary ghost stories. For example, while Franklin D. Roosevelt ran for president he had a radio program called "Fireside Chats." In that program he spoke directly to the American people. He broadcasted that show to nearly 40 million people. Jack Lule, author of "Understanding Media & Culture," also states that "'Fireside chats,' remain one of the most famous uses of radio in politics. Author of "The Rise of Radio" Marc Fisher, states "Radio has shaped American culture, the medium is always amorphous, changing to fit the zeitgeist of every year's consumer needs." Many people do not realize how radio has been a part of their lives and it should be recognized. Radio maybe one of the biggest inventions to revolutionize our media industry. Radio has had the power to influence many people and should be recognized as a powerful media outlet that impacted society.

The invention of the radio has impacted many people. It has had educational programs, entertainment programs, news, and music shows that many people listened to. Radio has helped create a great number of jobs for people and has given people a platform to share their views and ideas.

Work Cited

Almuhanna, Hamad. "How Radio Changed Our Lives." *How Radio Changed Our Lives.* N.p., 22
    Apr. 2013. Web. 14 Apr. 2015. Path: https://muhanna117.wordpress.com/2013/04/22/radio/.

"Becoming Modern: America in the 20's." *Radio*. National Humanities Center, n.d. Web. 14 Apr. 2015. Path: http://americainclass.org/sources//becomingmodern/machine/text5/text5.htm.

Fisher, Marc. "The Rise of Radio." *Washington Post*. Ed. Douglas Brinkley. Washington Post Company, 28 Jan. 2007. Web. 14 Apr. 2015.

Gugliotta, Guy. "How Radio Changed Everthing." *Discover*. Kalmbach Publishing Co, 31 May 2007. Web. 14 Apr. 2015. Path: http://discovermagazine.com/2007/jun/tireless-wireless.

Lule, Jack. "A New Kind of Mass Media." *Understanding Media and Culture: An Introduction to Mass Communication, v. 1.0.* Flat World Education, Mar. 2012. Web. 14 Apr. 2015.

Stefanyshyn, Deanna, and Julie Kendell. "The Influence of Radio and Television on Culture, Literacy and Education." *Text, Technologies – Community Weblog*. WordPres, 28 Oct. 2012. Web. 14 Apr. 2015.

APPENDIX

In this section, you will find all of the worksheets you need in order to complete your weekly assignments. This includes worksheets for scrapbook assignments, vocabulary, and journals. Make sure to use these worksheets and turn them in with your work as they are due. Refer to your syllabus for a schedule of due dates.

SCRAPBOOK ASSIGNMENT #1

Name_____

Choose your Scrapbook question/topic. Attach your first article to this page, and use the space here to write your response.

_____

_____

_____

_____

_____

_____

_____

_____

_____

SCRAPBOOK ASSIGNMENT #2

Name_____

Attach your article to this page, and use the space here to write your response.

_____

_____

_____

_____

_____

_____

_____

_____

_____

_____

_____

SCRAPBOOK ASSIGNMENT #3

Name_____

Attach your article to this page, and use the space here to write your response.

_____

_____

_____

_____

_____

_____

_____

_____

_____

_____

SCRAPBOOK ASSIGNMENT #4

Name_____

Attach your article to this page, and use the space here to write your response.

_____

_____

_____

_____

_____

_____

_____

_____

_____

_____

_____

SCRAPBOOK ASSIGNMENT #5

Name_____

Attach your article to this page, and use the space here to write your response.

_____

_____

_____

_____

_____

_____

_____

_____

_____

_____

SCRAPBOOK ASSIGNMENT #6

Name_____

Attach your article to this page, and use the space here to write your response.

_____

_____

_____

_____

_____

_____

_____

_____

_____

_____

SCRAPBOOK ASSIGNMENT #7

Name_____

Attach your article to this page, and use the space here to write your response.

_____

_____

_____

_____

_____

_____

_____

_____

_____

_____

_____

SCRAPBOOK ASSIGNMENT #8

Name_____

Attach your article to this page, and use the space here to write your response.

_____

_____

_____

_____

_____

_____

_____

_____

_____

_____

_____

SCRAPBOOK ASSIGNMENT #9

Name_____

Attach your article to this page, and use the space here to write your response.

_____

_____

_____

_____

_____

_____

_____

_____

_____

_____

SCRAPBOOK ASSIGNMENT #10

Name_____

Attach your article to this page, and use the space here to write your response.

_____

_____

_____

_____

_____

_____

_____

_____

_____

_____

SCRAPBOOK ASSIGNMENT #11

Name_____

Attach your article to this page, and use the space here to write your response.

_____

_____

_____

_____

_____

_____

_____

_____

_____

_____

_____

SCRAPBOOK ASSIGNMENT #12

Name_____

Attach your article to this page, and use the space here to write your response.

_____

_____

_____

_____

_____

_____

_____

_____

_____

_____

_____

VOCAB ASSIGNMENT #1

Name_____

Directions: For each word you have chosen, either (a) write out the full definition, (b) write a sentence using the word, or (c) compile a list of at least three synonyms and two antonyms for each word.

1. _____:_____
_____
_____
_____
_____

2. _____:_____
_____
_____
_____
_____

3. _____:_____
_____
_____
_____
_____

4. _____:_____
_____
_____
_____
_____

5. _____:_____
_____
_____
_____
_____

VOCAB ASSIGNMENT #2

Name_____

Directions: For each word you have chosen, either (a) write out the full definition, (b) write a sentence using the word, or (c) compile a list of at least three synonyms and two antonyms for each word.

1. _____:_____
_____
_____
_____
_____

2. _____:_____
_____
_____
_____
_____

3. _____:_____
_____
_____
_____
_____

4. _____:_____
_____
_____
_____
_____

5. _____:_____
_____
_____
_____
_____

VOCAB ASSIGNMENT #3

Name_____

Directions: For each word you have chosen, either (a) write out the full definition, (b) write a sentence using the word, or (c) compile a list of at least three synonyms and two antonyms for each word.

1. _____:_____
_____
_____
_____
_____

2. _____:_____
_____
_____
_____
_____

3. _____:_____
_____
_____
_____
_____

4. _____:_____
_____
_____
_____
_____

5. _____:_____
_____
_____
_____
_____

VOCAB ASSIGNMENT #4

Name_____

Directions: For each word you have chosen, either (a) write out the full definition, (b) write a sentence using the word, or (c) compile a list of at least three synonyms and two antonyms for each word.

1. _____:_____
_____
_____
_____
_____

2. _____:_____
_____
_____
_____
_____

3. _____:_____
_____
_____
_____
_____

4. _____:_____
_____
_____
_____
_____

5. _____:_____
_____
_____
_____
_____

VOCAB ASSIGNMENT #5

Name_____

Directions: For each word you have chosen, either (a) write out the full definition, (b) write a sentence using the word, or (c) compile a list of at least three synonyms and two antonyms for each word.

1. _____:_____
_____
_____
_____
_____

2. _____:_____
_____
_____
_____
_____

3. _____:_____
_____
_____
_____
_____

4. _____:_____
_____
_____
_____
_____

5. _____:_____
_____
_____
_____
_____

VOCAB ASSIGNMENT #6

Name_____

Directions: For each word you have chosen, either (a) write out the full definition, (b) write a sentence using the word, or (c) compile a list of at least three synonyms and two antonyms for each word.

1. _____:_____
_____
_____
_____
_____

2. _____:_____
_____
_____
_____
_____

3. _____:_____
_____
_____
_____
_____

4. _____:_____
_____
_____
_____
_____

5. _____:_____
_____
_____
_____
_____

VOCAB ASSIGNMENT #7

Name_____

Directions: For each word you have chosen, either (a) write out the full definition, (b) write a sentence using the word, or (c) compile a list of at least three synonyms and two antonyms for each word.

1. _____:_____
_____
_____
_____
_____

2. _____:_____
_____
_____
_____
_____

3. _____:_____
_____
_____
_____
_____

4. _____:_____
_____
_____
_____
_____

5. _____:_____
_____
_____
_____
_____

VOCAB ASSIGNMENT #8

Name_____

Directions: For each word you have chosen, either (a) write out the full definition, (b) write a sentence using the word, or (c) compile a list of at least three synonyms and two antonyms for each word.

1. _____:_____

_____

_____

_____

_____

2. _____:_____

_____

_____

_____

_____

3. _____:_____

_____

_____

_____

_____

4. _____:_____

_____

_____

_____

_____

5. _____:_____

_____

_____

_____

_____

VOCAB ASSIGNMENT #9

Name_____

Directions: For each word you have chosen, either (a) write out the full definition, (b) write a sentence using the word, or (c) compile a list of at least three synonyms and two antonyms for each word.

1. _____:_____
_____
_____
_____
_____

2. _____:_____
_____
_____
_____
_____

3. _____:_____
_____
_____
_____
_____

4. _____:_____
_____
_____
_____
_____

5. _____:_____
_____
_____
_____
_____

VOCAB ASSIGNMENT #10

Name_____

Directions: For each word you have chosen, either (a) write out the full definition, (b) write a sentence using the word, or (c) compile a list of at least three synonyms and two antonyms for each word.

1. _____:_____
_____
_____
_____
_____

2. _____:_____
_____
_____
_____
_____

3. _____:_____
_____
_____
_____
_____

4. _____:_____
_____
_____
_____
_____

5. _____:_____
_____
_____
_____
_____

VOCAB ASSIGNMENT #11

Name_____

Directions: For each word you have chosen, either (a) write out the full definition, (b) write a sentence using the word, or (c) compile a list of at least three synonyms and two antonyms for each word.

1. _____:_____
_____
_____
_____
_____

2. _____:_____
_____
_____
_____
_____

3. _____:_____
_____
_____
_____
_____

4. _____:_____
_____
_____
_____
_____

5. _____:_____
_____
_____
_____
_____

VOCAB ASSIGNMENT #12

Name_____

Directions: For each word you have chosen, either (a) write out the full definition, (b) write a sentence using the word, or (c) compile a list of at least three synonyms and two antonyms for each word.

1. _____:_____
_____
_____
_____
_____

2. _____:_____
_____
_____
_____
_____

3. _____:_____
_____
_____
_____
_____

4. _____:_____
_____
_____
_____
_____

5. _____:_____
_____
_____
_____
_____

JOURNAL ASSIGNMENT #1

Name_____

Use the space here to write your response to the journal question posed within the text.

_____

_____

_____

_____

_____

_____

_____

_____

_____

_____

JOURNAL ASSIGNMENT #2

Name_____

Use the space here to write your response to the journal question posed within the text.

_____

_____

_____

_____

_____

_____

_____

_____

_____

_____

JOURNAL ASSIGNMENT #3

Name_____

Use the space here to write your response to the journal question posed within the text.

_____

_____

_____

_____

_____

_____

_____

_____

_____

_____

_____

JOURNAL ASSIGNMENT #4

Name_____

Use the space here to write your response to the journal question posed within the text.

_____

_____

_____

_____

_____

_____

_____

_____

_____

_____

JOURNAL ASSIGNMENT #5

Name_____

Use the space here to write your response to the journal question posed within the text.

_____

_____

_____

_____

_____

_____

_____

_____

_____

_____

Name of Editor: _____Name of Author: _____

Essay # _____   Essay Type: _____

DIRECTIONS:

1. Identify the topic/thesis statement.
2. Identify any grammatical mistakes.
3. Identify any awkward or wordy sentences. Attempt to rewrite a few for better flow.
4. Write a note on content; does it flow/have logic? Does it meet requirements?

1. Thesis Statement: _____

   _____

   _____

2. Grammatical Mistakes: Make marks and/or notations within the text

3. Style: Rewrite sentences here.

   _____

   _____

   _____

   _____

   _____

   _____

   _____

   _____

   _____

4. Note on Content: _____

_____

_____

_____

_____

_____

_____

_____

_____

Name of Editor: _____Name of Author: _____

Essay # _____   Essay Type: _____

DIRECTIONS:

1. Identify the topic/thesis statement.
2. Identify any grammatical mistakes.
3. Identify any awkward or wordy sentences. Attempt to rewrite a few for better flow.
4. Write a note on content; does it flow/have logic? Does it meet requirements?

1. Thesis Statement: _____

_____

_____

2. Grammatical Mistakes: Make marks and/or notations within the text

3. Style: Rewrite sentences here.

_____

_____

_____

_____

_____

_____

_____

_____

4. Note on Content: _____

_____

_____

_____

_____

_____

_____

_____

Name of Editor: _____Name of Author: _____

Essay # _____   Essay Type: _____

DIRECTIONS:

1. Identify the topic/thesis statement.
2. Identify any grammatical mistakes.
3. Identify any awkward or wordy sentences. Attempt to rewrite a few for better flow.
4. Write a note on content; does it flow/have logic? Does it meet requirements?

1. Thesis Statement: _____

   _____

   _____

2. Grammatical Mistakes: Make marks and/or notations within the text

3. Style: Rewrite sentences here.

   _____

   _____

   _____

   _____

   _____

   _____

   _____

   _____

   _____

4. Note on Content: _____

_____

_____

_____

_____

_____

_____

_____

Name of Editor: _____ Name of Author: _____

Essay # _____   Essay Type: _____

DIRECTIONS:

1. Identify the topic/thesis statement.
2. Identify any grammatical mistakes.
3. Identify any awkward or wordy sentences. Attempt to rewrite a few for better flow.
4. Write a note on content; does it flow/have logic? Does it meet requirements?

1. Thesis Statement: _____

    _____

    _____

2. Grammatical Mistakes: Make marks and/or notations within the text

3. Style: Rewrite sentences here.

    _____

    _____

    _____

    _____

    _____

    _____

    _____

    _____

4. Note on Content: _____

_____

_____

_____

_____

_____

_____

_____

Name of Editor: _____ Name of Author: _____

Essay # _____   Essay Type: _____

DIRECTIONS:

1. Identify the topic/thesis statement.
2. Identify any grammatical mistakes.
3. Identify any awkward or wordy sentences. Attempt to rewrite a few for better flow.
4. Write a note on content; does it flow/have logic? Does it meet requirements?

1. Thesis Statement: _____

_____

_____

2. Grammatical Mistakes: Make marks and/or notations within the text

3. Style: Rewrite sentences here.

_____

_____

_____

_____

_____

_____

_____

4. Note on Content: _____

_____

_____

_____

_____

_____

_____

_____

Name of Editor: _____Name of Author: _____

Essay # _____   Essay Type: _____

DIRECTIONS:

1. Identify the topic/thesis statement.
2. Identify any grammatical mistakes.
3. Identify any awkward or wordy sentences. Attempt to rewrite a few for better flow.
4. Write a note on content; does it flow/have logic? Does it meet requirements?

1. Thesis Statement: _____

   _____

   _____

2. Grammatical Mistakes: Make marks and/or notations within the text

3. Style: Rewrite sentences here.

   _____

   _____

   _____

   _____

   _____

   _____

   _____

   _____

   _____

4. Note on Content: _____

_____

_____

_____

_____

_____

_____

_____